HIKE
THE SANTA MONICA MOUNTAINS

Hike. Contemplate what makes you happy and what makes you happier still. Follow a trail or blaze a new one. **Hike.** Think about what you can do to expand your life and someone else's. **Hike.** Slow down. Gear up. **Hike.** Connect with friends. Re-connect with nature.

Hike. Shed stress. Feel blessed. **Hike** to remember. **Hike** to forget. **Hike** for recovery. **Hike** for discovery. **Hike.** Enjoy the beauty of providence. **Hike.** Share the way, The Hiker's Way, on the long and winding trail we call life.

HIKE
THE SANTA MONICA MOUNTAINS

BY
JOHN MCKINNEY

TheTrailmaster.com

HIKE The Santa Monica Mountains By John McKinney

HIKE The Santa Monica Mountains © 2019 The Trailmaster, Inc. All rights reserved. No part of this book may be used or reproduced in any manner whatsoever without written permission except in the case of brief quotations embodied in articles and reviews.

Acknowledgments: For three decades worth of cooperation, field- and fact-checking, a huge Trailmaster thank you to the rangers and administrators of the California Department of Parks & Recreation, the Santa Monica Mountains National Recreation Area, and the Santa Monica Mountains Conservancy. And Milt McAuley, Sage of the Chaparral, we'll always remember you. Thanks for inspiring so many to hike the Santa Monica Mountains.

ISBN-13: 978-0-934161-77-0
Book design by Lisa DeSpain
Cartography by Tom Harrison, TomHarrisonMaps.com
Cover photo by Chuck Graham
Photo Credits: California State Parks pp. 23, 91; Bob Howells p. 102; National Park Service pp. 54, 77. Backbone Trail maps (pp. 136, 138, 140) courtesy of National Park Service.
HIKE Series Editor: Cheri Rae

Published by Olympus Press and The Trailmaster, Inc. www.TheTrailmaster.com (Visit our site for a complete listing of all Trailmaster publications, products, and services.)

Although The Trailmaster, Inc. and the author have made every attempt to ensure that information in this book is accurate, they are not responsible for any loss, damage, injury, or inconvenience that may occur to you while using this information. You are responsible for your own safety; the fact that an activity or trail is described in this book does not mean it will be safe for you. Trail conditions can change from day to day; always check local conditions and know your limitations.

Contents

Introduction 11

HIKE the Santa Monica Mountains 14

Santa Monica Mountains
EAST

WILL ROGERS STATE HISTORIC PARK 21
   Tour Cowboy Philosopher's home, trek to Inspiration Point

RUSTIC CANYON 25
   A surprisingly rugged little enclave, every bit as woodsy and secluded as its name suggests

RUSTIC CANYON STAIRS 28
   Stairway to haven, 500 steps and a short hike into some weird history

SULLIVAN CANYON 31
   A gem of a canyon. Choose an easy walk or moderate loop. Outstanding views

TEMESCAL CANYON 35
   Grand gateway to mountains leads to oak-shaded canyon, lovely waterfall, vistas from Skull Rock

LOS LIONES CANYON & THE OVERLOOK 39
   Fab views via a favorite Palisades path for celeb-sighting, socializing and sunset-watching

TOPANGA STATE PARK..43
   Eagle Rock, Eagle Springs and highlights of "the
   largest state park within a city limit in the U.S."

TOPANGA STATE PARK TO WILL ROGERS......................47
   A one-way hike (mostly downhill!) on a grand length
   of the Backbone Trail

MULHOLLAND GATEWAY...53
   Caballero Canyon and a grand entrance to the valley-
   side of the Santa Monicas

Santa Monica Mountains
CENTRAL

HONDO CANYON...59
   "Deep" Canyon, pinkish-hued rock formations and a
   sterling stretch of Backbone Trail

CALABASAS PEAK & RED ROCK CANYON...........................63
   Step into the American Southwest: Red sandstone
   outcroppings sculpted by wind and water

COLD CREEK PRESERVE...67
   An off-the-beaten path preserve and one of Southern
   California's most pristine free-flowing creeks

SADDLE PEAK..71
   Splendid stretch of Backbone Trail travels botanically
   intriguing Dark Canyon. Inspiring vistas from cloud-
   topping summit

KING GILLETTE RANCH...75
   From the new visitors center for the Santa Monica
   Mountains, hit the trail to Inspiration Point

MALIBU CREEK*...79
   Classic, must-do hike to Goat Buttes, Century Lake
   and the M*A*S*H site

REAGAN RANCH* 83
   Rolling meadows, grand old oaks, a trail to the Chief

CASTRO CREST & THE GRAND TOUR* 87
   Backbone Trail adventure and grand tour of Malibu
   Creek State Park

LAS VIRGENES VIEW PARK* 93
   Grand vistas of the central portion of the Santa
   Monica Mountains

NEWTON CANYON FALLS 97
   Easy access to a lovely little cascade

Santa Monica Mountains
WEST

SOLSTICE CANYON* 99
   Easy hike through tranquil canyon, recovering from
   wildfire and inviting once more

ZUMA CANYON* 105
   Challenging hike on and off the trail through one of
   range's most rugged canyons

CHARMLEE PARK* 109
   Wildflower walks and ocean vistas from Malibu bluffs.
   Plenty of easy paths!

NICHOLAS FLAT* 113
   Inspiring ocean vistas and flowers galore on the way to
   a peaceful pond. A Trailmaster favorite!

SANDSTONE PEAK 117
   Circle X Ranch and remarkable vistas from the high
   point of the Santa Monicas

*Recovering from 2018 Woolsey Fire

Rancho Sierra Vista Satwiwa 121
    Sycamore Canyon Falls and a hike through the homeland of the Chumash

Sycamore Canyon 125
    Monarch butterflies and finest sycamore grove in the state park system. Easy and moderate trail options

La Jolla Canyon 129
    Explore Point Mugu State Park backcountry: Rugged canyon, peaceful pond and native grassland

Mugu Peak 133
    Views of ocean waves and waves of grass from the wild west end of the mountains

Backbone Trail 137
    Fifty years in the making, the marquee trail of the mountains

About the Author 142

Wildflowers, waterfalls and wonderful scenery that has been the backdrop for countless movies and TV shows are highlights for hikers.

HIKE ON.

Bordered by two of the busiest freeways in the world—the Ventura and the San Diego—they remain a near-wilderness. Within easy reach of 16 million people, they nevertheless offer solitude and plenty of silent places.

Introduction

Literally and figuratively, the Santa Monica Mountains are my home mountains.

As a young adult I lived in the most urban section of the Santa Monica Mountains—the Hollywood Hills—and in one of the most rural parts—Topanga Canyon.

The home mountains are where I camped overnight with the scouts and learned to drive a car with a clutch. Later in life, the home mountains helped me unwind from the stresses of metropolitan life.

Going back to the 1980s, I've helped defend the home mountains from unwise developments, cheered supporters and chastised bureaucrats, celebrated new parklands and new trails. I even spent the greater part of a year mapping, promoting, and speaking out for the Backbone Trail, the 65-mile pathway that extends across the spine of the range.

All of which means I have a particular fondness for hiking the Santa Monica Mountains and delight in sharing my favorite trails. Wildflowers, waterfalls and wonderful scenery that's been the backdrop for hundreds of movies and thousands of episodes of TV shows are highlights for hikers.

Spring wildflower blooms are impressive. A hike to Nicholas Flat might reveal wishbone bush, encelia, chia, Parry's phacelia, ground-pink, scarlet bugler, goldfields…check out the "What's Blooming?" section of the Santa Monica Mountains National Recreation Area website.

Trails lead by still waters—Nicholas Pond, Century Lake and Charmlee's Old Reservoir—and by lively creeks in Sullivan Canyon, Malibu Canyon and Zuma Canyon. Behold surprising waterfalls in Temescal Canyon, Sycamore Canyon and La Jolla Canyon.

More movies and TV shows have been filmed in the Santa Monica Mountains than anywhere else in the world, and it's lots of fun to hike to and through movie locations. Malibu Creek State Park, just to name one park, has served as Wales, Korea, Connecticut, and even the Planet of the Apes. Other park sites in the mountains have subbed for the Wild West, Italy, Switzerland, Asia, outer space, and a variety of fantasy locations. More than 500 productions a year take place in these mountains.

Because M*A*S*H, both the original movie and the long-running television series, was filmed here, and because what is now parkland used to be a movie

Introduction

ranch, Malibu Creek is the state park most associated with the film industry. Thousands of visitors a year hike out to the original site of the M*A*S*H filming.

We who love hiking in these mountains are forever grateful to Milt McAuley, who wrote trail guides and the classic *Wildflowers of the Santa Monica Mountains*. "Come on an adventure, walk the trails," urged McAuley, who hiked until shortly before his death at the age of 89. "Experience the beauty and friendship that is waiting for you."

Hike smart, reconnect with nature and have a wonderful time on the trail.

Hike on.
–John McKinney

Author John McKinney says: "Get inspired by these mountains on a hike to Inspiration Point."

Santa Monica Mountains

Bordered by two of the busiest freeways in the world—the Ventura and San Diego—they remain a near-wilderness. Within easy reach of 16 million people, they nevertheless offer solitude and plenty of silent places.

Geography

The Santa Monica Mountains is the only relatively undeveloped mountain range in the U.S. that bisects a major metropolitan area. The mountains extend from Griffith Park in the heart of Los Angeles to Point Mugu, 50 miles away. The range is 12 miles wide at its broadest point, and reaches an elevation of about 3,000 feet.

One of the few east-west trending ranges in the country, the Santa Monica Mountains can cause a little geographic confusion to the first-time visitor. Santa Monica Bay and the Malibu coastline also extend from east to west alongside the mountains so that the mountain explorer actually looks south to the ocean and heads west when hiking up-coast.

Natural Attractions

The mountains host a Mediterranean ecosystem, the only one in the country under National Park Service protection. Large stretches are open and natural, covered with chaparral and oak trees, bright in spring with wildflowers. Oak woodland and fern glens shade gentle seasonal creeks.

Largest areas of open space are in the western part of the mountains. Point Mugu State Park holds one of the finest native tall-grass prairies and one of the best sycamore groves in the state. The gorge sculpted by Malibu Creek is an unforgettable sight.

In the eastern portion of the mountains, open space is harder to come by, but those pockets that do exist are all the more valuable because they are so close to the metropolis. Canyons such as Los Liones, Caballero, Rustic and Sullivan are precious resources.

History

Ancestors of the Chumash Indians lived in the mountains as early as 7,000 years ago. Abundant food sources helped the Chumash become the largest Indian tribal group in California at the time of Juan Cabrillo's arrival in 1542. The Chumash's highly developed culture included oceangoing plank canoes called *tomols* and a system of astronomy that was both mystical and practical.

Spanish missionaries, soldiers and settlers displaced the Chumash. During the 19th century, the Santa Monicas were controlled by a few large land holdings—including Rancho Topanga-Malibu-Sequit—and used primarily for cattle ranching. As the land holdings were broken up, some ranchers supplemented their modest living by renting space to visiting horseback riders and vacationers.

Conservationists proposed Whitestone National Park in the 1930s and Toyon National Park in the 1960s, but it wasn't until Will Rogers, Topanga, Malibu Creek and Point Mugu state parks were established in the late 1960s that the mountains received any substantial government protection. In 1978 the

Outstanding Conservationists: Ruth Kilday, "Mother of the Backbone Trail," and Joe Edmiston, executive director of the Santa Monica Mountains Conservancy.

bill creating Santa Monica Mountains National Recreation Area was approved by Congress.

Administration

Some 70,000 acres of public land is preserved within the boundaries of the Santa Monica Mountains National Recreation Area. This represents about one-third of the 200,000 acres covered by the range.

The National Recreation Area is not one large area, but a patchwork of state, federal and county land, as well as private property still to be acquired. The major land stewards are California State Parks and the National Park Service.

For three decades the Santa Monica Mountains Conservancy, a state agency, has been particularly effective at acquiring parkland in the mountains. The Mountains Recreation and Conservation Authority manages and provides ranger services for parks that it owns and are owned by the Santa Monica Mountains Conservancy.

Hike into Topanga State Park, "the largest state park within a city limit in the U.S."

EVERY TRAIL TELLS A STORY.

Santa Monica Mountains

East

HIKE ON.

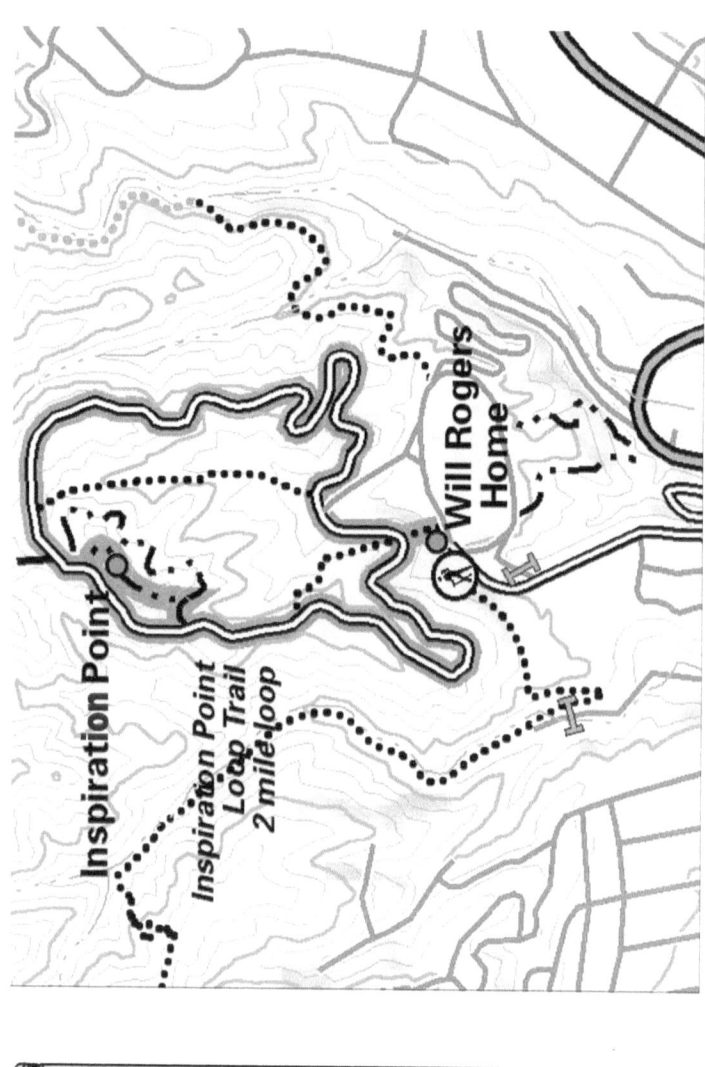

TheTrailmaster.com

WILL ROGERS STATE HISTORIC PARK

INSPIRATION POINT LOOP TRAIL

To Inspiration Point is 2 miles round trip with a 300-foot elevation gain

Will Rogers, often called the "Cowboy Philosopher," bought a spread in the Santa Monica Mountains in 1922. He and his family enlarged their weekend cottage to 31 rooms, including 11 baths and 7 fireplaces.

The Oklahoma-born Rogers toured the country as a trick roper, punctuating his act with humorous comments on the news of the day. His roping act led the humorist to later fame as a newspaper columnist, radio commentator and movie star.

Today, the ranch and grounds of the Rogers Ranch is maintained as Will Rogers State Historic Park, set aside in 1944. View a short film on Rogers' life at the park visitor center and tour the ranch house, still filled with his prized possessions.

Come for the history, stay for the hiking; there's a lot here for hikers. Rogers himself designed the riding trails that wind into the hills behind his ranch. The path to Inspiration Point is an easy walk for the whole family.

The park is the eastern terminus for the Backbone Trail that extends some 65 miles across the spine of the Santa Monica Mountains to Point Mugu State Park. Extend the hike to Inspiration Point and get great views by ascending the first mile or so of the Backbone Trail. One of The Trailmaster's favorite lengths of the Backbone connects Topanga and Will Rogers state parks; it's about 11 miles one-way.

DIRECTIONS: From Sunset Boulevard in Pacific Palisades, 4.5 miles inland from Sunset's junction with Pacific Coast Highway, turn inland on the access road leading to Will Rogers State Historic Park. Park your car near the polo field or near Rogers' house.

THE HIKE: Begin at the Will Rogers home and join the path up the hill to the west of the ranch house and left of the tennis courts. Follow the zigzag path 0.1 mile to meet Inspiration Point Loop Trail (a wide dirt fire road). The trail bends west, offering vistas of Santa Monica Bay, then heads north into the mountains. The path ascends a ridge overlooking nearby Rivas Canyon and leads to a junction, 0.8 mile from the trailhead.

Bear right to Inspiration Point, not really a point at all, it's actually more of a flat-topped knoll. Nevertheless, clear-day views are inspiring: Santa Monica Bay, the metropolis, San Gabriel Mountains, Catalina.

(From the signed junction below Inspiration Point, consider an optional exploration on famed Backbone Trail. Ascend Chicken Ridge (one mile with nearly 500 feet in elevation gain) and enjoy more great views of the mountains, metropolis and wide blue Pacific.)

Return to the main loop and continue your clockwise tour, first continuing northeast, then east and then descending south. The lower length of trail, lined with eucalyptus, leads back to the polo grounds and visitor center.

Will Rogers and his family loved riding the mountain trails

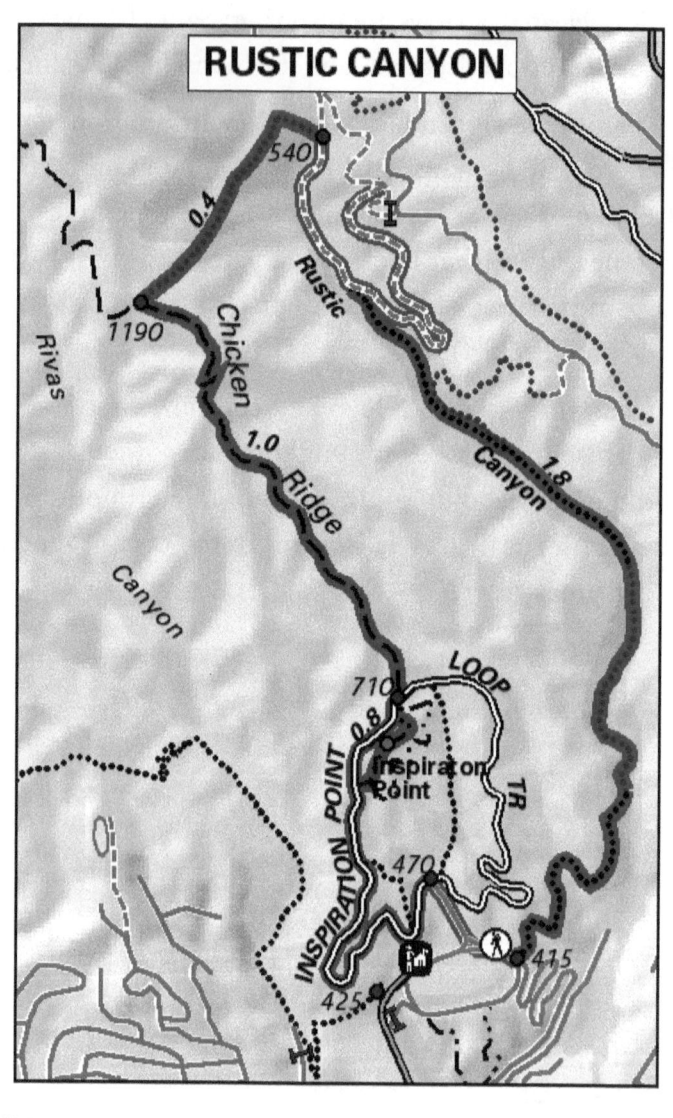

TheTrailmaster.com

Rustic Canyon

Inspiration Point Loop, Backbone, Rustic Canyon Trails

Loop through Will Rogers State Historic Park and Rustic Canyon is 4.75 miles round trip with 900-foot elevation gain

Rustic Canyon is every bit as woodsy and secluded as its name suggests. The surprisingly rugged little enclave is wild, narrow and steep, with dramatic rock walls.

Rustic Canyon has a storied past. In the late 19th Century, the Santa Monica Forestry Station was established adjacent to the canyon. The many eucalyptus in and around the canyon are a result of tobacco millionaire-builder of Venice-forestry pioneer Abbot Kinney's efforts.

Most of Rustic Canyon remained undeveloped until the 1920s when it became the retreat of a group of Los Angeles businessmen known as The Uplifters, who enjoyed good fellowship and "uplifted" the arts.

One of the canyon's stranger sights is a substantial wrought-iron gate, one-time entrance to Murphy Ranch, believed to have been a compound run by Nazi sympathizers during the 1930s.

A top natural attraction of Rustic Canyon is Rustic Creek. Most mountain watercourses flow only after rains, but Rustic Creek is one of the few that's spring-fed and thus usually flows all year round.

This hike begins in Will Rogers State Historic Park. You'll follow the trail to Inspiration Point, march a mile or two up the Backbone Trail, then descend into Rustic Canyon and loop back to Will Rogers.

DIRECTIONS: From Sunset Boulevard in Pacific Palisades, 4.5 miles inland from Sunset's junction with Pacific Coast Highway, turn inland on the access road leading to Will Rogers State Historic Park. For this hike, park in the easternmost part of the lot near the picnic area.

THE HIKE: From Will Rogers home, on the east side of a wide field, take the paved road (or parallel dirt path) leading past a line of eucalyptus trees. Sometimes called Polo Trail, this path leads to the park's riding ring and to the start of the east branch of Inspiration Point Loop Trail, also signed as Backbone Trail.

About 0.8 mile from the trailhead, reach a signed junction below Inspiration Point. Detour to Inspiration Point for inspiring clear-day views of the city if you wish, but this hike continues with famed Backbone Trail. Climbing Chicken Ridge, the path offers great views of downtown, Century City, the sweep of Santa Monica Bay and Catalina Island. After a mile's climb along the ridge, the trail reaches a junction.

Turn sharply to the right and begin a steep 0.5-mile descent on a manzanita-lined connector trail to the bottom of Rustic Canyon. Left, up-canyon, leads to Camp Josepho, a Boy Scout camp, and to a junction with Sullivan Ridge Fire Road.

Bear right, down-canyon, on the path, which stays at the canyon bottom, crossing and re-crossing the creek. Pass the ruins of small homes that have suffered the ravages of fire and flood. Canyon flora includes the usual riparian growth plus stray exotics including cactus, aloe, jade, periwinkle and lots of German ivy.

At about the 3.5-mile mark, pass a small dam, and soon the trail narrows and the canyon walls close in. Nearing the main part of the state park, the canyon opens up and you bear right on a wide trail which bends uphill toward the polo field and you'll follow an elaborate trail, supported with wooden trestles, cross a bridge over a culvert, and return to the parking lot and Rogers' home where you began the hike.

RUSTIC CANYON STAIRS

L.A. boasts some fascinating stairway walks, but only one drops into the wilds of the Santa Monica Mountains. If you're up for the challenge of a 23-story down-and-up workout, you'll like this unique hike into Rustic Canyon.

Begin this short hike (1 mile round trip with 250-foot elevation gain) by walking a brief length of dirt road, to where a paved road begins. A gate operated by the Boy Scouts' Camp Josepho limits traffic along, so traffic is sparse. It's a 15-minute walk or so to the stairs. Keep an eye out for a chain-link fence on the left side of road, and then a break in the fence. Follow a 30-foot dirt path to where the stairs are located.

Take the 500 or so stairs down to bottom of Rustic Canyon. In places it's reminiscent of hiking around the hill towns in Italy or the Cinque Terre, where stairways are common along the sentiero (trail).

If you feel like you're taking baby steps, well, you are. Compared to typical stairs measuring 7.75 inches, the Rustic Canyon stairs have a short rise of 5.5 inches. Nevertheless it adds up to a lot of elevation lost and gained—more than 230 feet—like walking up and down the stairs in a 23-story building.

The stairs are punctuated by various flat landings at irregular increments, from which you can admire the view of Rustic Canyon with its wild, narrow, steep and dramatic rock walls on the way down and catch your breath on the way back up.

A short path leads to the trail at the bottom of Rustic Canyon. (See the hike account in this guide.) Climb back up the stairs to improved cardiovascular health and Sullivan Ridge.

A bit more walking up the paved road leads to a substantial wrought-iron gate and a crumbling flagstone wall, the one-time entrance to Murphy Ranch, believed to have been a compound run by Nazi sympathizers during the 1930s. The Rustic Canyon explorer will find creepy burned-out and graffiti-marred remains of concrete and steel structures.

If you're up for real hike, with the reward of grand mountain and metropolitan views, a dirt road extends 5 more miles along Sullivan Ridge to the crest of the Santa Monica Mountains and Mulholland Drive.

DIRECTIONS: From Sunset Boulevard in Pacific Palisades, just opposite the Riviera Country Club, turn north on Capri Drive and drive 0.6 mile to a junction with Casale Road; bear right and hunt for street parking. Walk 150 yards along parking restricted Capri Drive to its end and the beginning of Sullivan Canyon Ridge fire road.

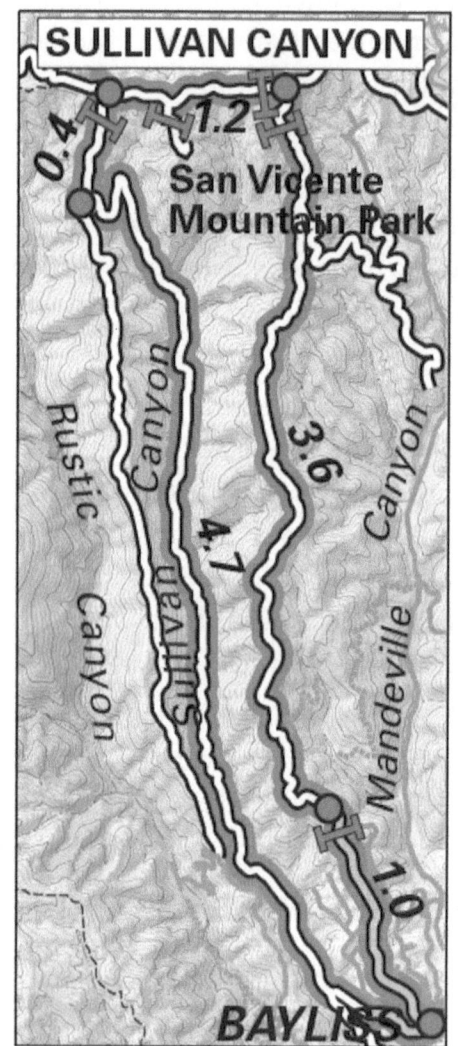

Sullivan Canyon

Sullivan Canyon Trail

10-mile loop with 1,200-foot elevation gain

Sullivan Canyon is one of the gems of the eastern portion of the Santa Monica Mountains. Stately oaks and sycamores shade a seasonal creek and a fine trail travels the length of the canyon.

The canyon was very attractive to its former owner—the Los Angeles County Sanitation District—and was long near the top of the list as a potential landfill site; protests by environmentalists derailed the dump.

Sullivan's high and narrow canyon walls display handsome sandstone outcroppings, as well as a blue-gray bedrock known as Santa Monica slate. During winter and spring, canyon walls are colored with clusters of ceanothus.

Casual walkers will enjoy a nearly flat stroll a mile or three along the canyon floor. More energetic hikers will make a loop trip by climbing out of the canyon to Mulholland Drive and San Vicente Mountain Park and Nike Site. The retired radar tower now provides visitors with 360-degree views of the Santa Monica Mountains, the San Fernando Valley, and the L.A. Basin. BTW, it's an outstanding place to watch the sunset—one of the best in the Southland.

DIRECTIONS: From the San Diego Freeway (405) in west Los Angeles, exit on Sunset Boulevard and head west 2.5 miles to Mandeville Canyon Road. Turn right and, after 0.25 mile, turn left on Westridge Road. Travel 1.2 miles to Bayliss Road. Make a left, continue 0.25 mile, make another left on Queensferry Road, and look for the trailhead at road's end. You'll need to park on Bayliss Road; not along the 100 yards closest to the trailhead, though, because it's posted "No Parking, 7AM to 7PM."

THE HIKE: Walk past a green gate and down an asphalt service road (closed to vehicles) to the bottom of Sullivan Canyon. Head right on the wide trail, which meanders near a willowy streambed, beneath the boughs of antiquarian oaks and across carpets of lemon grass.

The tranquil trail climbs very gently. At the 3.5-mile mark, the main Sullivan Canyon bends right to the northeast while the road ascends northwest up a smaller side canyon.

After an intense climb, reach a junction with Sullivan Ridge Fire Road. Go right (north) on a more mellow 0.4-mile ascent to Mulholland Drive. Follow dirt Mulholland east 1.2 miles along the ridge to San Vicente Mountain Park.

The park features interpretive displays that explain how, from 1956 to 1958, this isolated perch served as one of the Los Angeles area Nike-Ajax anti-aircraft missile launch sites.

Enjoy fabulous views from the vista points, then head south on Westridge Fire Road and partake of more vistas of both mountains and metropolis from the ridge separating Sullivan and Mandeville canyons. After a mostly downhill 3.6-mile jaunt from San Vicente Mountain Park, you'll arrive at a small parking lot for the Westridge Trailhead and meet paved Westridge Road.

Descend a half mile to Bayliss Road, turn right and walk another half mile to Queensferry Road. Turn right and return to the trailhead.

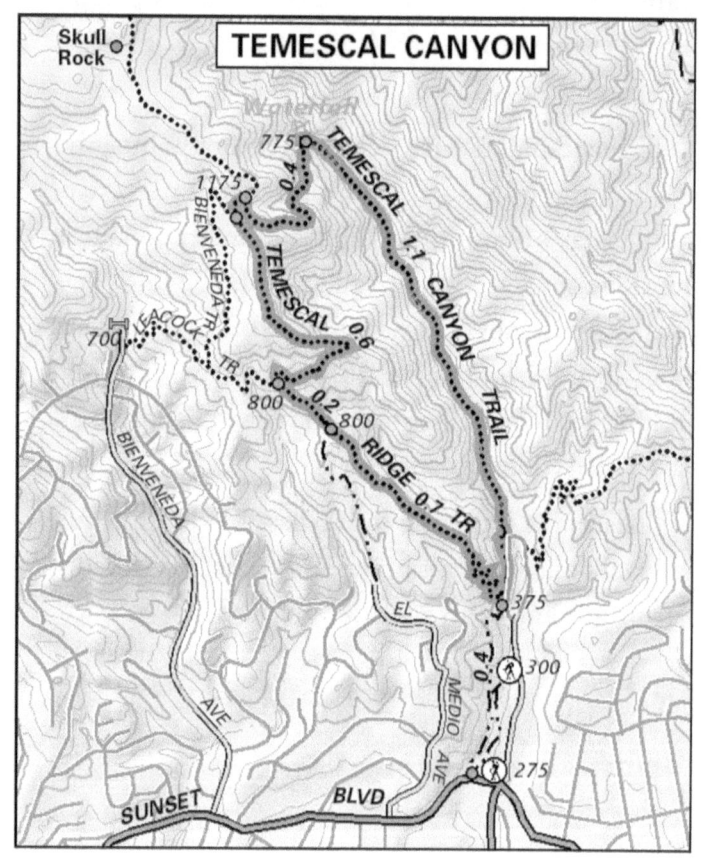

TEMESCAL CANYON

TEMESCAL CANYON

Canyon loop is 3.8 miles round trip with 900 foot elevation gain

I have a particular fondness for Temescal Gateway Park in Pacific Palisades. Not only does this park have it all (restrooms, picnic grounds, water fountains and more), park pathways quickly leave it all behind.

Temescal Canyon is an ideal Santa Monica Mountains sampler. You get an oak- and sycamore-shaded canyon, a seasonal waterfall and terrific views from the ridge crest.

You'll escape civilization but not other hikers; the canyon is a very popular place to hike.

Sidewalks, picnic grounds, and an intermittent greenbelt along Temescal Canyon Road might tempt intrepid hikers to stride the mile from the beach to the trailhead.

Temescal has long been a canyon that inspired nature lovers and enlightenment-seekers. During the 1920s and 1930s, the canyon hosted Chautauqua assemblies—large educational and recreational gatherings that featured lectures, concerts and stage performances.

The canyon was purchased by the Presbyterian Synod in 1943 and used as a retreat center until 1995 when the Santa Monica Mountains Conservancy acquired it.

Outdoor education programs for children are held at Temescal Gateway Park. Temescal Canyon Conference and Retreat Center features the notably designed Elizabeth Cheadle Dining Hall and offers overnight accommodations for up to 100 people.

DIRECTIONS: From Los Angeles, head west on the Santa Monica Freeway (10) to its end and continue up-coast on Pacific Coast Highway. Turn north (right) on Temescal Canyon Road and drive 1.1 miles. Just after the intersection with Sunset Boulevard, turn left into the lower parking area (fee) for Temescal Gateway Park.

You can also locate free parking along Sunset Boulevard or along Temescal Canyon Road and walk into Temescal Gateway Park.

THE HIKE: Walk up-canyon on the landscaped path past the restrooms. The footpath takes on a wilder appearance and soon crosses a branch of Temescal Creek via a wooden footbridge.

At a signed junction, save Temescal Ridge Trail for your return route and continue through the canyon on Temescal Canyon Trail. Travel among graceful old oaks, maples and sycamores to the "doggie turnaround" (no dogs beyond this point) and enter Topanga State Park.

The path ascends moderately to another footbridge and a close-up view of the small waterfall, tumbling over some large boulders. Leaving the canyon behind, the path steepens and climbs westward up Temescal Ridge to a signed junction with Temescal Ridge Trail.

(I always enjoy heading uphill on this trail a half mile or so to distinctly shaped Skull Rock, a good place to rest, cool off, and admire the view.)

As you return to the trailhead down Temescal Ridge Trail, you'll get excellent views of Santa Monica Bay, Palos Verdes Peninsula, Catalina Island, and downtown Los Angeles.

The path descends steeply and tunnels into tall chaparral. Continue past junctions with Bienveneda and Leacock trails and follow the narrow ridgeline back to a junction with Temescal Canyon Trail. Retrace your steps back to the trailhead.

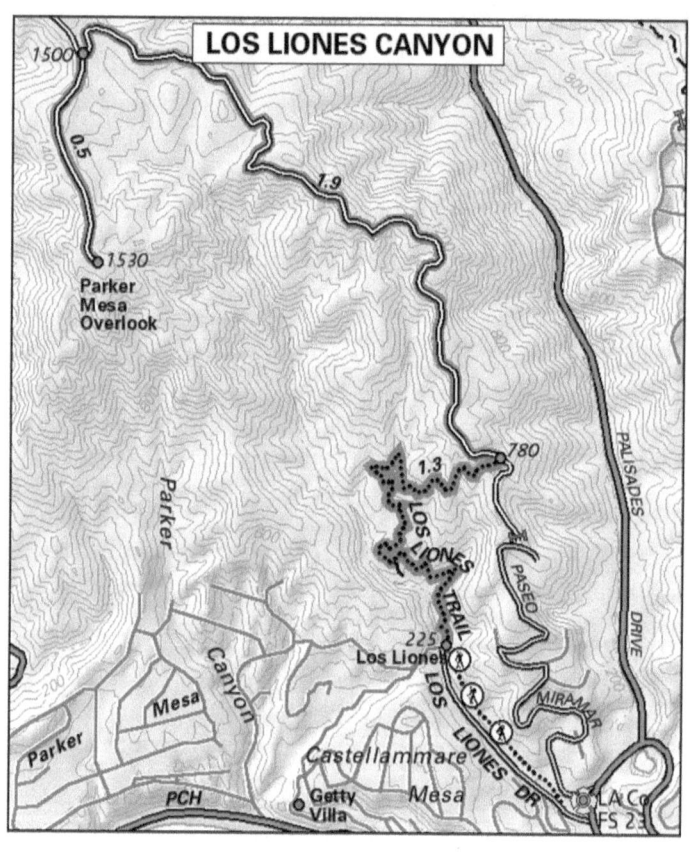

Los Liones Canyon & Parker Mesa Overlook

Los Liones Canyon, East Topanga Fire Road Trails

From Los Liones Drive to The Overlook is 6 miles round trip with 1,500-foot elevation gain

Rugged Los Liones Canyon is but a mile from Sunset Boulevard, but very much apart from the Westside city scene. "The Overlook" offers grand views of West Los Angeles and Santa Monica Bay.

This hike explores the coastal slopes of Topanga State Park. Your goal is a viewpoint sometimes called Parker Mesa Overlook, sometimes called Topanga Overlook, but most often simply called The Overlook. Views of West Los Angeles and the sweep of Santa Monica Bay are superb. Sunset (the descending day star not the winding boulevard) views are often inspiring.

Hikers heading for The Overlook are among the most sociable of sojourners. This hike is known for its high number of celebrity sightings—which I cannot confirm, un-hip hiker that I am.

Two trails help you reach the inspiring view. Los Liones Canyon Trail travels through its namesake canyon to East Topanga Fire Road which in turn leads to The Overlook. Or head directly for The Overlook via the fire road.

Many hikers choose to start this hike by driving way up winding Paseo Miramar high into the Palisades. East Topanga Trailhead, a.k.a. Paseo Miramar Trailhead is a more popular trailhead for hiking to The Overlook than you'd imagine, considering the one at Los Liones has much better parking.

From The Overlook, the ambitious hiker can trek into the main part of Topanga State Park.

DIRECTIONS: From Pacific Coast Highway in Pacific Palisades, turn inland on Sunset Boulevard for 0.25 mile. Turn left on Los Liones Drive and follow it a half mile to a church, a bend in the road and a small trailhead parking area for ten cars. (Don't park in the adjacent church lot.)

Below the trailhead on Los Liones Drive are other parking areas, one with restrooms. Plus there is additional parking along the road itself.

THE HIKE: Follow the trail into the canyon. After 0.25 mile, the trail begins to climb in earnest, switchbacking through the chaparral.

After leveling out for a stretch, the path then switchbacks even more earnestly through thickets of ceanothus. Los Liones Trail intersects East Topanga Fire Road about 0.25-mile from that road's beginning at Paseo Miramar.

Turn left (northwest) on the fire road and continue your ascent. The road travels a cool, north slope and you get good over-the-right-shoulder views of neighboring Santa Ynez Canyon, a canyon that's wild and dramatic in its upper reaches (in the state park) and thoroughly subdivided in its lower reaches.

A two-mile ascent along the fire road brings you to a junction with a trail leading south along a bald ridge. Join this trail and hike 0.5-mile to The Overlook.

Enjoy panoramas of Westside L.A., Santa Monica Bay, Palos Verdes and Catalina Island.

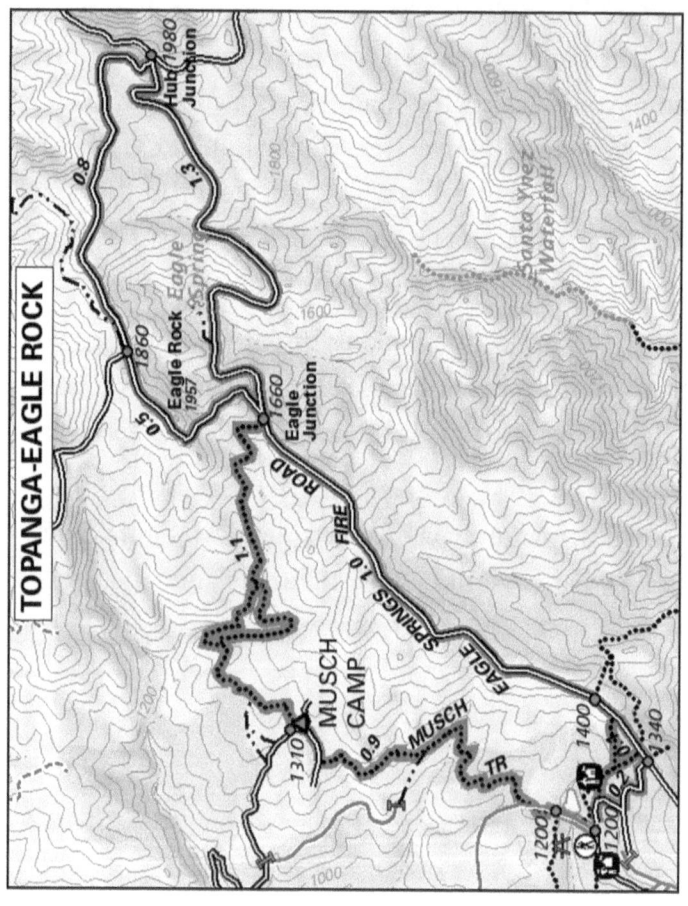

Topanga State Park

Eagle Springs Fire Road
(Backbone Trail)

To Eagle Rock via Eagle Rock/Eagle Springs Loop is 6.5 miles round trip with 800-foot elevation gain

Topanga Canyon is a quiet retreat, surrounded by L.A. sprawl but retaining its rural character. The state park is sometimes billed as "the largest state park within a city limit in the U.S."

The name Topanga is from the Shoshonean Indian dialect. Until the 1880s, there was little permanent habitation in the canyon. Early settlers tended vineyards, orchards, and cattle ranches.

In the 1920s, the canyon became a popular weekend destination for Los Angeles residents. Summer cabins were built along Topanga Creek and in surrounding hills. For $1 round trip fare, tourists could board a Packard auto stage in Santa Monica and be driven up Pacific Coast Highway and Topanga Canyon Road to the canyon's scenic spots.

Most Topanga trails are good fire roads. In the heart of the state park, the hiker will discover Eagle Rock, Eagle Spring and get topographically oriented to Topanga.

I have a particular fondness for Topanga Canyon, having resided there and hiked there often during my grad school days. The park definitely offers four-season hiking: On a blustery winter day, city and canyon views are superb, in springtime, the hillsides are colored with wildflowers, and autumn offers great hiking weather and clear-day vistas.

Summer, too, has its charms. It's doubtful any poets will rhapsodize about such summer bloomers as bur-sage, mugwort, Indian milkweed, chaparral pea or ashyleaf buckwheat, though the scarlet petals of the California fuchsia and the tiny pink petals of the slim aster do have a certain charm. Just get an early start!

DIRECTIONS: From Topanga Canyon Boulevard, turn east on Entrada Road; that's to the right if you're coming from Pacific Coast Highway. Follow Entrada Road by turning left at every opportunity until you arrive at Topanga State Park. The trailhead is at the end of the parking lot.

THE HIKE: From the Topanga State Park parking lot, follow the distinct trail eastward to a signed junction, where you'll begin hiking on Eagle Springs Road. You'll pass through an oak woodland and through chaparral country. The trail slowly and steadily gains about 800 feet in elevation on the way to Eagle Rock. When you reach a junction, bear left on the north loop of Eagle Springs Road to Eagle Rock. A short detour will bring you to the top of the rock.

To complete the loop, bear sharply right (southwest) at the next junction, following the fire road as it winds down to Eagle Spring. Past the spring, you return to Eagle Spring Road and retrace your steps back to the trailhead.

Three-mile long Musch Ranch Trail, which passes from hot chaparral to shady oak woodland, crosses a bridge and passes the park pond, is another fine way to return to the trailhead.

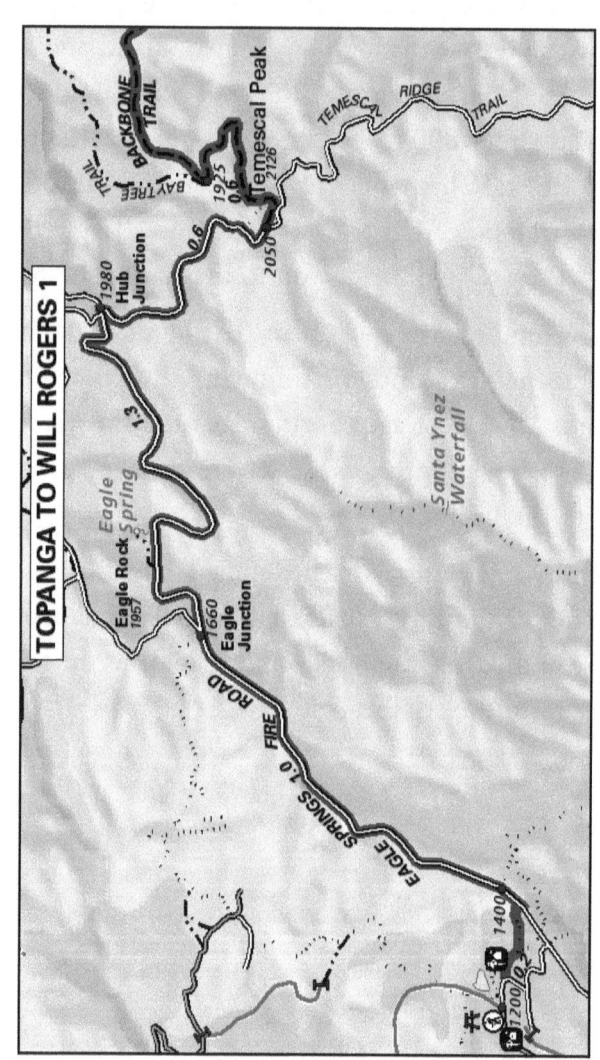

TOPANGA TO WILL ROGERS

BACKBONE TRAIL

From Topanga SP to Will Rogers SHP is 10.5 miles one way with 1,800-foot elevation loss

Here's your chance to hike a length of the majestic Backbone Trail that extends 65 miles across the Santa Monica Mountains. The Backbone Trail has been a dream of hikers since the 1950s; to date all but 3 miles of trail have been constructed.

The trail extends west from Will Rogers State Historic Park across the spine of the range to Point Mugu State Park. The section from Will Rogers to Topanga State Parks was one of the first sections of the Backbone Trail completed. I first did this hike in the late 1970s, and I still love it, and recommend it as a great introduction to the marquee trail of the mountains.

The lower reaches of the trail offer a fine tour of the wild side of Topanga Canyon while the ridgetop sections offer far-reaching inland and ocean views.

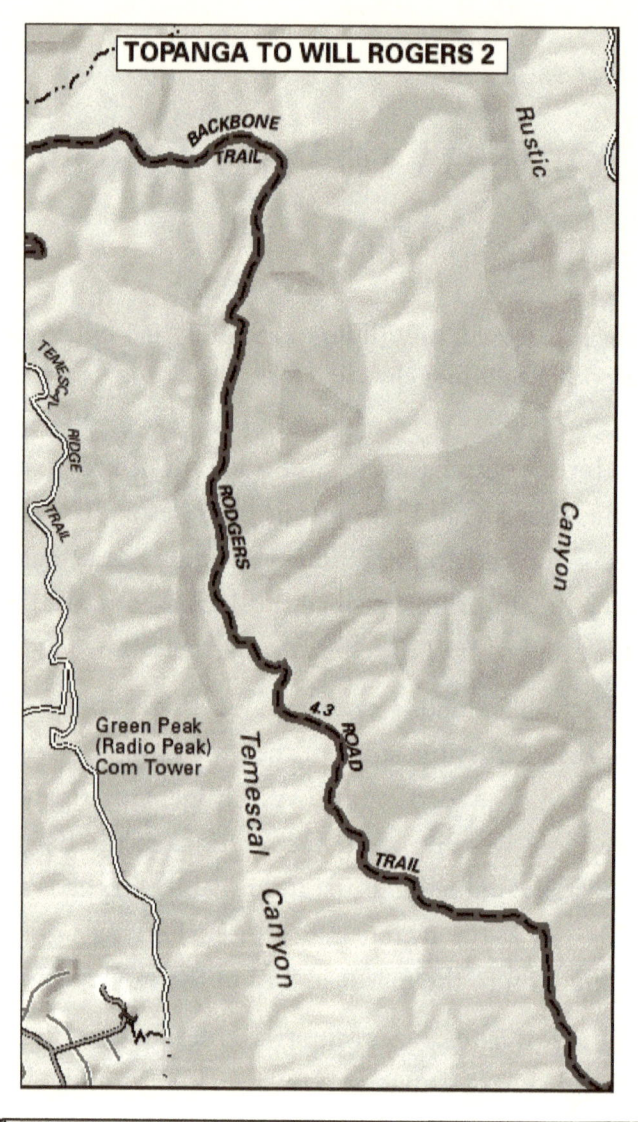

It's a one-way hike, more downhill than uphill, with a manageable car shuttle.

DIRECTIONS: From Topanga Canyon Boulevard, turn east on Entrada Road; that's to the right if you're coming from Pacific Coast Highway. Follow Entrada Road by turning left at every opportunity until you arrive at Topanga State Park. The trailhead is at the end of the parking lot.

To Will Rogers State Historic Park: From Sunset Boulevard in Pacific Palisades, 4.5 miles inland from Pacific Coast Highway, turn inland on the signed park access road.

THE HIKE: From the Topanga SP parking lot, follow the distinct trail eastward to a signed junction, where you'll begin hiking on Eagle Springs Road. A one-mile ascent brings you to Eagle Junction and the signed Backbone Trail. Follow the Backbone past Eagle Spring and reach the park's main intersection, aptly called Hub Junction, 1.3 miles from Eagle Junction.

Continue with the Backbone Trail, heading south 0.6 mile to another junction near Temescal Peak; the fire road continues south as Temescal Ridge Trail but you stick with the Backbone Trail curving east then north another 0.6 mile to a junction with Bay Tree Trail on your left.

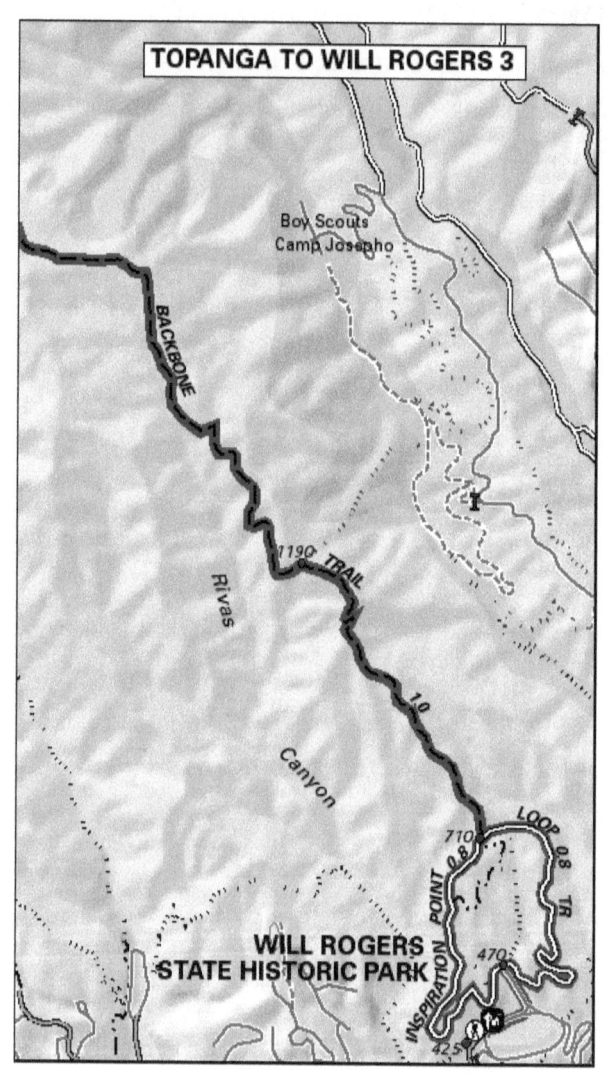

Stick with the Backbone (Rogers Road) and follow the dirt road (really more like a trail). As you make the long descent (5.3 more miles and a 1,200-foot elevation loss) to a junction with the Inspiration Point Loop Trail) savor the views: To the left is Rustic Canyon and the crest of the mountains near Mulholland Drive. To the right, Rivas Canyon descends toward the sea.

Follow either branch of the loop trail (also signed as the Backbone Trail) and descend to the parking area in Will Rogers State Historic Park.

The Topanga-Will Rogers Backbone Trail segment has been a hit with hikers for more than 40 years.

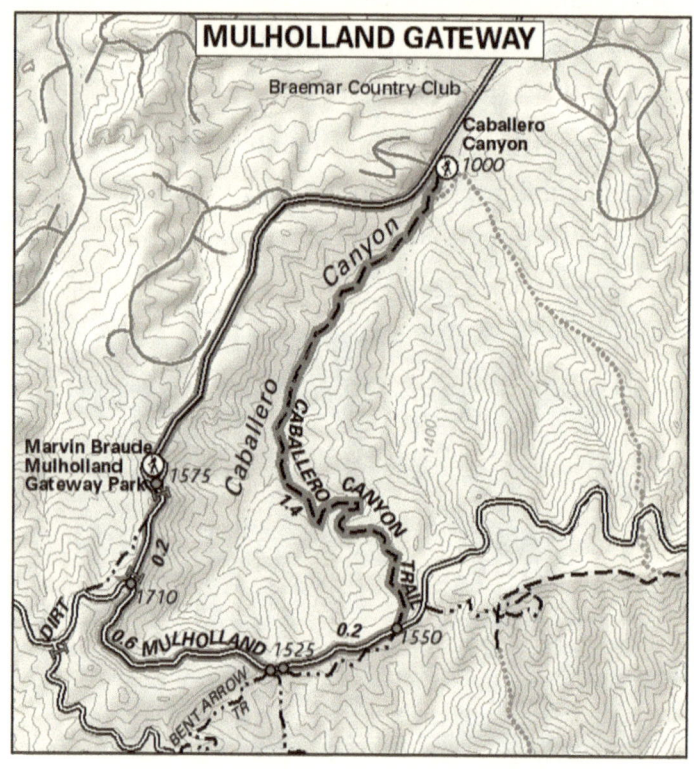

MULHOLLAND GATEWAY

CABALLERO CANYON TRAIL

To Mulholland Drive is 2.8 miles round trip with 550-foot elevation gain; return via Mulholland Gateway Park is 3.5 miles round trip

Caballero Canyon Trail seems like one of those trails constructed as an afterthought after the completion of a large upscale residential housing development. Actually, though, the trail was in place and a favorite of hikers who dwell on the valley side of the Santa Monicas before all those haciendas went up alongside upper Reseda Boulevard.

Such valley-side trailheads are precious. While the Santa Monica Mountains are scarcely three miles as the red-tailed hawk flies from the valley-crossing Ventura Freeway (one of the busiest in the world), few would-be hikers exit the autobahn and head for the hills. This paucity of foot traffic in part has resulted from a lack of valley-side trailheads, attractive or otherwise.

While Caballero Canyon Trailhead is modest indeed, Marvin Braude Mulholland Gateway Park, located just up the road, is a trailhead deluxe: water fountains, toilets, parking. Two grassy hillsides offer superb picnic sites. A walkway leads around a native plant landscaped vista point, where a dozen handsome rock benches offer places to contemplate the mountains above and metropolis below.

Park namesake and longtime Los Angeles city councilman Marvin Braude was an inspirational and influential supporter of Santa Monica Mountains parklands. The "Mulholland Gateway" in the park name is apropos, too, because a long, unpaved section of famed Mulholland Drive is easy to access from the trailhead. Mountain bikers like to incorporate the dirt byway (most of which is closed to vehicles) into long rides along the crest of the

For nearly a century, motorists have driven Mulholland to reach mountain parks and trails.

range and hikers find it useful for bridging the gap between canyons.

DIRECTIONS: From the Ventura Freeway (Highway 101) in Tarzana, exit on Reseda Boulevard and head north 2 miles to the Caballero Canyon Trailhead, located on the east side of the boulevard nearly opposite the entrance to the Braemar Country Club. Find free parking along the boulevard or continue to road's end at Mulholland Gateway Park (fee parking).

THE HIKE: The dirt path descends past a worn trailhead kiosk and travels along a sycamore-lined seasonal creek more or less parallel to Reseda Boulevard. The path climbs south through the chaparral toward the mountains.

About a mile out, the trail zigzags and enters Topanga State Park, then climbs some more to a bench located just below Mulholland Drive that offers a place to sit and contemplate metropolitan views. Return the same way or via a slightly longer route that takes in a bit of Mulholland Drive.

At dirt Mulholland, bear right (west). After 0.2 mile you'll pass junctions with the faint Rustic Canyon Trail and with Bent Arrow Trail, then continue another 0.6 mile to a signed junction above Mulholland Gateway Park.

Descend 0.2 mile to the park. Join the locals out for their exercise and follow the sidewalk alongside Reseda Boulevard back to the trailhead.

Malibu Gorge: a scene to remember, and a popular film location since the silent movie days.

EVERY TRAIL TELLS A STORY.

Santa Monica Mountains
Central

HIKE ON.

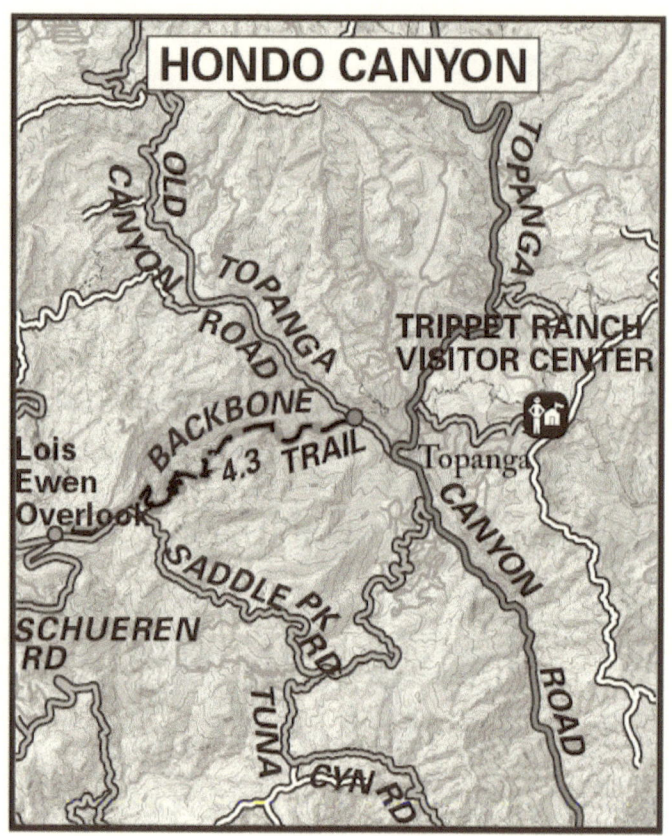

Hondo Canyon

Backbone Trail

From Saddle Peak Road to Topanga Canyon is 4.5 miles one way with 1,200-foot elevation loss

"With the possible exception of Zuma Canyon, Hondo is the most dramatic canyon in the mountains," states Ron Webster, who designed the footpath through Hondo Canyon.

One look over the canyon rim at Hondo (which means "deep" in Spanish) will convince most hikers that this trail is no walk in the park. Attractions along the way include pinkish-hued sedimentary rock formations and a handsome gorge, oak woodland and tall chaparral.

The Hondo Canyon hike can be a 4.5-mile one way, mostly downhill jaunt from Schueren Road to Topanga State Park or a 9-mile round trip adventure. The trailhead on Old Topanga Road is close to Topanga Center.

While the trail was being built, Hondo Canyon experienced fire, flood, and even the Northridge Earthquake. Signs of seismic activity from the quake were dramatic. Large trees at the bottom of Hondo Canyon were bowled over by huge boulders dislodged from the canyon walls. Other trees remained standing, minus limbs and chunks of trunk, after surviving the rock fusillade.

DIRECTIONS: To reach the Topanga State Park trailhead, exit the Ventura Freeway (101) in Woodland Hills on Topanga Canyon Boulevard and proceed south. Note the state park entrance on your left and continue 0.25 mile more to Old Topanga Canyon Road, turning right, and proceeding another 0.25 mile to the signed Backbone Trail that departs from the west side of the road. Find (scarce) parking along the road.

To reach the Saddle Peak Road trailhead: From the intersection of Topanga Canyon Boulevard and Old Topanga Road, proceed 5.5 miles up the latter road to Mulholland Highway. Turn left and drive 4.5 miles to Stunt Road, turn left, and continue 4 more miles to a junction with Schueren Road. Park off Stunt Road (which assumes a new name—Saddle Peak Road and continues east) in one of the wide dirt turnouts.

THE HIKE: Begin at the yellow fire gate on the north side of Stunt Road. Walk one hundred yards and look rightward for the footpath. Follow the ridgetop long known informally as Fossil Ridge. Embedded in a pink-hued rock are what appear to be giant clam fossils.

After traveling the ridge for about 0.6 mile, the trail drops off the ridgetop. Enjoy clear-day views of the Warner Center area of the San Fernando Valley, then lose sight of civilization with the descent into Hondo Canyon. Flower lovers will note the abundant tree poppy, bush lupine and mariposa lily growing on this slope.

The trail drops to the bottom of the canyon, cool in the shade of bay laurel, oak and sycamore. A seasonal stream and waterfall at the canyon bottom come to life after a good rain. The path climbs briefly along the south canyon wall, then descends past evidence of the great quake of 1994, including shattered oaks and dislodged boulders located near the mouth of the canyon.

The path crosses lush Topanga Meadows. Winter rains can make meadow trails mighty mucky. Expect a couple pounds of mud to glom onto your hiking boots. Soon after crossing the meadow, the trail leads across creek and to the trailhead on Old Topanga Road.

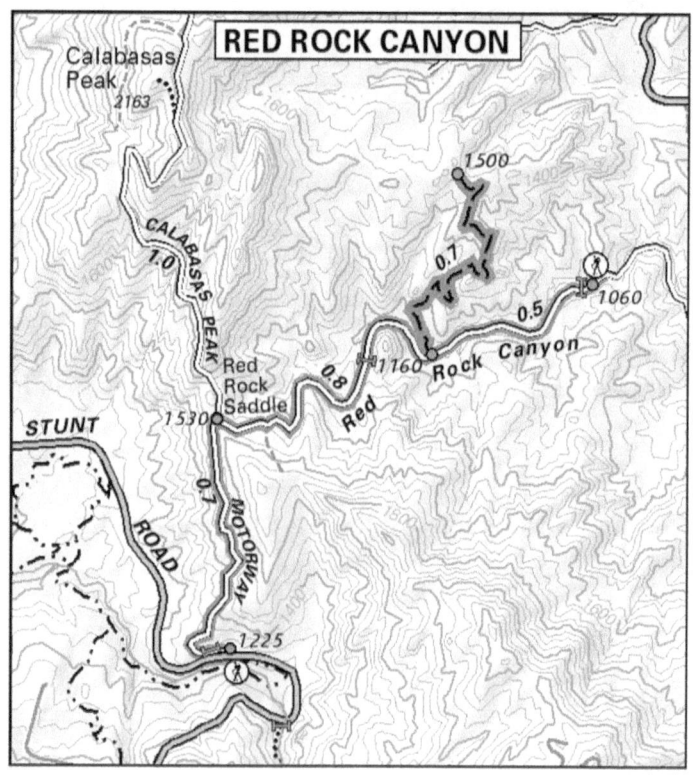

CALABASAS PEAK & RED ROCK CANYON

CALABASAS PEAK, RED ROCK CANYON TRAILS

From Stunt Road to Calabasas Peak is 3.8 miles round trip with 900-foot elevation gain; to Red Rock Canyon Park is 4.4 miles round trip with 600-foot gain

Towering red rocks, along with floral clouds of white and blue-hued ceanothus are among the attractions of Red Rock Canyon Park near Topanga Canyon. The rocks are joined by colorful wildflowers in the spring, including cliff aster, clarkia, golden bush and many more blooms.

Check out red sandstone outcroppings reminiscent of the American Southwest and ascend Calabasas Peak (2,163 feet) for great clear-day views of the Santa Monica Mountains, San Fernando Valley and the San Gabriel Mountains. And/or hike to Red Rock Canyon Park, which offers drinking water and a small picnic area but is otherwise undeveloped.

DIRECTIONS: From the Ventura Freeway (Highway 101) in Calabasas, exit on Las Virgenes Road and travel 3.25 miles south to Mulholland Highway. Turn left (east) and proceed four miles to Stunt Road, bear right and drive exactly a mile to the parking area on the right side of Stunt Road. The trailhead is on the left side of Stunt Road by road paddle "1.0".

To reach Red Rock Canyon Park directly by road, exit the Ventura Freeway in Woodland Hills on Topanga Canyon Road and head south a mile to Mulholland Highway. Turn west and drive 2.2 miles to Old Topanga Canyon Road. Head 3.6 miles south, then turn west on narrow Red Rock Road. Drive 0.8 miles (the last 0.2 miles are unpaved) to Red Rock Canyon Park.

THE HIKE: Ascend north on the Calabasas Peak Motorway Trail. Behind you is a view of Cold Creek Canyon, one of the treasures of the Santa Monica Mountains. Trail-side geology is fascinating: large, tilted slabs and fins of sandstone have been sculpted by erosion into weird shapes.

Bordering the fire road are chaparral-blanketed slopes dominated by toyon, laurel sumac, mountain mahogany and ceanothus. These larger shrubs are joined by a host of smaller ones including buckwheat, black sage, bush sunflowers and sagebrush.

About 0.7 mile from the trailhead is a saddle, where powerlines cross the road, sometimes known as Red Rock Saddle, and a junction.

(The left-forking road is a continuation of Calabasas Peak Motorway and leads another mile to the top of a ridge. A left-branching path leads directly to the peak.)

Rest a while at the bench at the saddle, then take the right fork and begin a 0.7-mile long descent to the bottom of Red Rock Canyon. The canyon narrows and appears more and more intriguing as you near the bottom.

At the 1.5-mile mark, signed Red Rock Canyon Trail offers an intriguing option. The northbound footpath crosses a trickle of a creek and climbs among the rock formations on the north wall of the canyon. Trail's end is at an overlook.

The major trail continues along the canyon bottom another 0.5 mile to the heart of Red Rock Canyon Park. It's worth extending your hike with a short stroll among the impressive red-rock formations stacked up along the dirt segment of this road that leads to the park entry road.

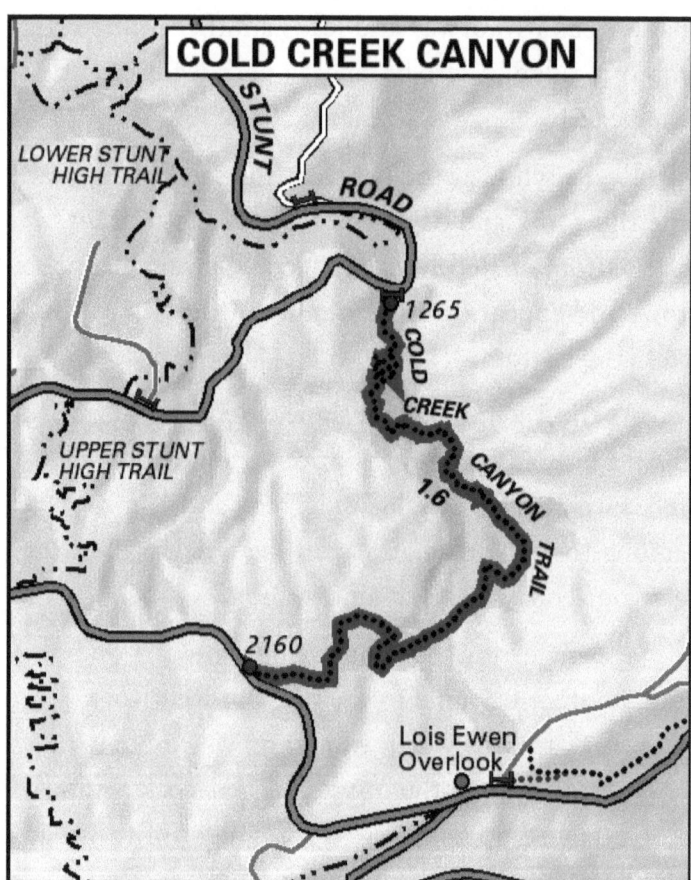

COLD CREEK PRESERVE
COLD CREEK TRAIL

To Lower Gate on Saddle Road is 3.2 miles round trip with 900-foot elevation gain

Cold Creek Canyon is one of the secret treasures of the Santa Monica Mountains. A year-round stream and a protected north-facing canyon nurture a rich variety of ferns and flowering plants in the 1,600-acre Cold Creek Preserve.

For decades, hiker access to Cold Creek has been ever-changing and, at times, problematic. Latest issue is an invasion of the New Zealand mud snail. Before you go, contact the Mountain Restoration Trust (818-591-1701, mountainstrust.org) for the latest trails information or to join one of the excellent interpretive walks led by Cold Creek Docents.

Cold Creek Canyon was once part of a ranch, homesteaded in the early years of this century. It later served as a ranch/retreat for the Murphy family who donated their ranch to the Nature Conservancy in

1970s, stipulating that Cold Creek be forever preserved in its natural state. The Nature Conservancy later transferred stewardship to the Mountains Restoration Trust.

The natural world of Cold Creek Canyon is diverse. Lining Cold Creek are ferns, flowers and cattails. Winter rains swell the creek, creating a dozen small waterfalls.

A hundred bird species have been sighted within the preserve, including golden eagles. Hikers may encounter a squirrel raccoon, deer or even a bobcat.

Wildflower-lovers will find much to admire. Early bloomers (February to April) include the white blossoms of the milkmaid. Later in spring, look for the bright yellow canyon sunflower and the yellow-orange spotted Humboldt lily.

Remember that this is an upside-down hike; the elevation gain occurs during your return.

DIRECTIONS: From the Ventura Freeway (101) in Calabasas, exit on Las Virgenes Road. Head south to Mulholland Highway, turn east and continue to Stunt Road. Turn right and drive 3.43 miles (watch the road paddles for mileage indicators) to the signed Cold Creek Preserve entrance on your left. A chain link fence marks the preserve boundary and you'll spot a fire hydrant near the entrance gate.

THE HIKE: Head through the gate and down the trail. One of the first shrubs you'll encounter along the trail is red shank, a floral cousin to the far more prolific chamise. You'll recognize it by its characteristic peeling bark. It's a late bloomer—August is its prime time.

After a half-mile of travel, you'll pass a bridge over Cold Creek. An old Dodge pickup truck mired in the middle of the trail suggests that the path used to be a road. Occasional breaks in the brush offer views of Calabasas Peak dead-ahead, and a sandstone formation to the right known as Fossil Ridge.

As the path, shaded by oak and bay, nears the canyon bottom, the vegetation becomes more lush. Woodwardia and bracken ferns thrive along Cold Creek. The towering sandstone walls that form Cold Creek absorb rainfall, then slowly release water throughout the year.

A bit more than a mile from the trailhead is the remains of an old house. Sandstone boulders formed the walls of the structure. Quite an ingenious use of materials at hand.

Beyond the rock house, the trail drops steeply into a marshy world of ferns and Humboldt lilies. You'll cross Cold Creek on a wooden footbridge. The trail leads uphill for a time, then returns to the creek. Trail's end is at the preserve's lower gate on Stunt Road.

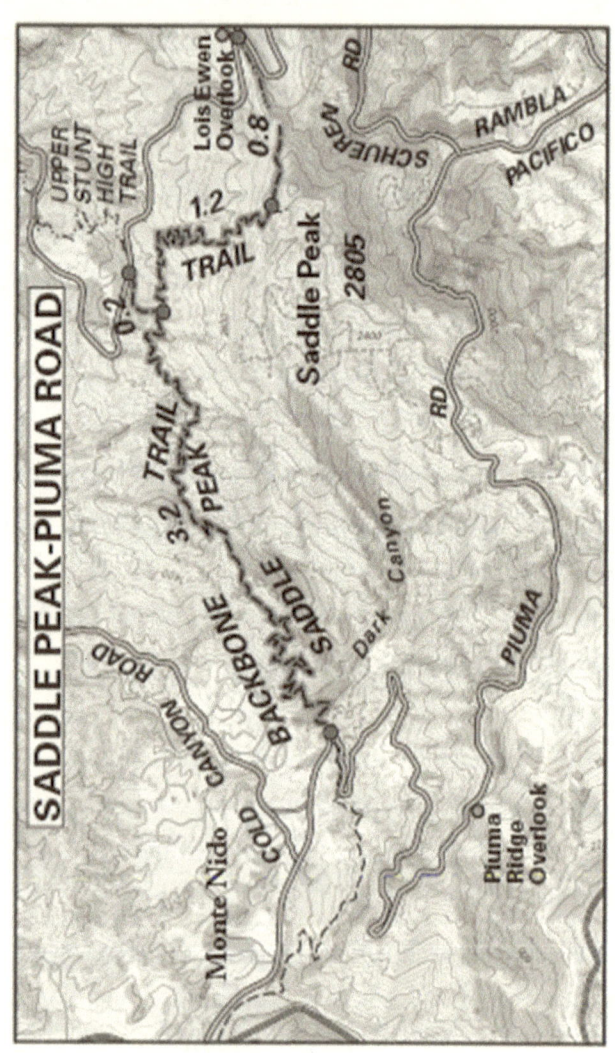

Saddle Peak

Backbone Trail

From Piuma Road to Saddle Peak is 9.2 miles round trip with 2000-foot gain

Handsome sandstone formations, commanding coastal and metropolitan views, and botanically intriguing Dark Canyon are some of the highlights of a hike to Saddle Peak. A superb stretch of Backbone Trail crosses the boulder-strewn crest of the mountains east of Malibu Creek State Park and leads to the peak.

The peak, actually two peaks with a "saddle" in between, is one of the highest points in the central part of the Santa Monica Mountains. Saddle Peak West is forested with communications antennae and off-limits to hikers. Saddle Peak East isn't a real looker, but is an easy summit climb and offers great vistas.

The commanding promontory stands about 2,800 feet high and often pokes above the coastal clouds that blanket lesser peaks and ridges. Located only about 2.5 miles as the cliff swallows (look for these birds among the peak's sandstone outcroppings) fly from the coast, Saddle Peak is a superb perch for gazing out at Santa Monica Bay and the Channel Islands. Eastern views include downtown Los Angeles and Mt. San Jacinto.

Expect a vigorous workout on the Backbone Trail from Piuma Road to Saddle Peak. (When a trail gains 500 feet or more in a mile, I automatically classify it as "strenuous.") One highlight of this hike is Dark Canyon, a lovely retreat with quiet pools shaded by bay and alder. (For a shorter, more family-friendly jaunt to Saddle Peak, take a hike from Stunt Road.)

DIRECTIONS: From the Ventura Freeway (Highway 101) in Agoura, exit on Las Virgenes Road and drive 4.7 miles south to Piuma Road. Turn left and drive 1.2 miles (0.2 mile past Piuma's intersection with Cold Canyon Road) to the signed trailhead, close to road paddle 1.19.

THE HIKE: From Piuma Road, the Backbone Trail drops into Dark Canyon. Ferns, Humboldt lily and tangles of a rare native grape thrive in the canyon bottom.

Leave behind the cool, moist sycamore- and alder-shaded canyon and begin a long, switchbacking ascent among ceanothus and manzanita. When you pause to catch your breath on this earnest ascent, look back to admire a dramatic view to the west:

Malibu Creek State Park and the impressive canyon cut by its namesake creek.

The trail winds among great boulders, which frame views of Cold Creek Canyon to the northeast and Calabasas Peak to the north. About 2.2 miles from the trailhead, you'll pass a minor saddle and small meadow, then continue another mile to intersect the connector trail leading down to Saddle Peak Road.

Continue past this junction on the Backbone Trail, which ascends Saddle Peak's brush-covered slopes, brightened in the cooler months by the bright red berries of the toyon.

The path meanders among bold sandstone outcroppings then continues climbing to a junction. About 1.2 miles from the previous junction, leave the Backbone Trail and ascend the connector path right (south) 0.1 mile to a dirt road. Go left to the top of East Peak or right to the saddle of Saddle Peak and enjoy the views.

King Gillette Ranch

Inspiration Point Trail

From Visitor Center to Inspiration Point is 1 mile round trip with 200-foot elevation gain

Anthony C. Beilenson Visitor Center, located in the King Gillette Ranch just east of Malibu Creek State Park, features a state-of-the-art photovoltaic solar energy system, and is the National Park Service's first "Net Zero" visitor center—powered entirely by its own energy.

Built entirely of recycled materials, the center was constructed from the existing ranch stables. Inside, visitors learn about the region's unique Mediterranean ecosystem, rich movie history, and the many recreation opportunities available in the mountains. It's an interagency effort, meaning that in addition to the National Park Service, all the major players in the mountains are represented, including the Santa Monica Mountains Conservancy, the Mountains

Recreation and Conservation Authority and California State Parks.

The ranch was once home to safety razor magnate King Camp Gillette and boasts a 1928 Spanish Colonial Revival mansion designed by renowned architect Wallace Neff. Movie director Clarence Brown bought the ranch, followed by the Claretian Order of the Catholic Church, the Church Universal and Triumphant and Soka University.

The 588-acre ranch became public parkland in 2007. Along with a number of buildings, classic and not, the ranch includes a long eucalyptus-lined entry road, a large pond and wide lawns. And then there's the wild side of the ranch—grasslands, scrub-dotted slopes and woodlands with valley oak and coast live oak.

No doubt a more extensive trail network will emerge at the ranch; meanwhile get started with the short hike to Inspiration Point, a knoll with 360-degree vistas.

DIRECTIONS: From the Ventura Freeway (Highway 101) exit on Las Virgenes Road and drive south three miles to Mulholland Highway. Turn left and almost immediately take a right into the signed King Gillette Ranch. Drive down the long and lovely entrance road to the visitor center on the right.

THE HIKE: Walk the landscaped pathway on the south side of the lot back to the entrance road and go right, crossing a bridge over Stokes Creek. Bear right at a road junction and walk over a short causeway over the pond. Stay to right of a building and meet two dirt paths behind it.

Continue straight on the rougher, steeper trail. (The more distinct path contours around the knoll and curves west.)

A short but aggressive ascent leads to Inspiration Point and views of the towering rocks above Malibu Gorge and the Gillette Mansion and sprawling ranch. Continue along the trail a short distance to a split.

Ridge Trail leads south along the ridge, but you descend eastward on a mellow descent over oak-dotted slopes. Wander around the Gillette Mansion and improvise a route past the pond back to the visitor center.

Learn all about the Santa Monica Mountains at this state-of-the-art visitor center.

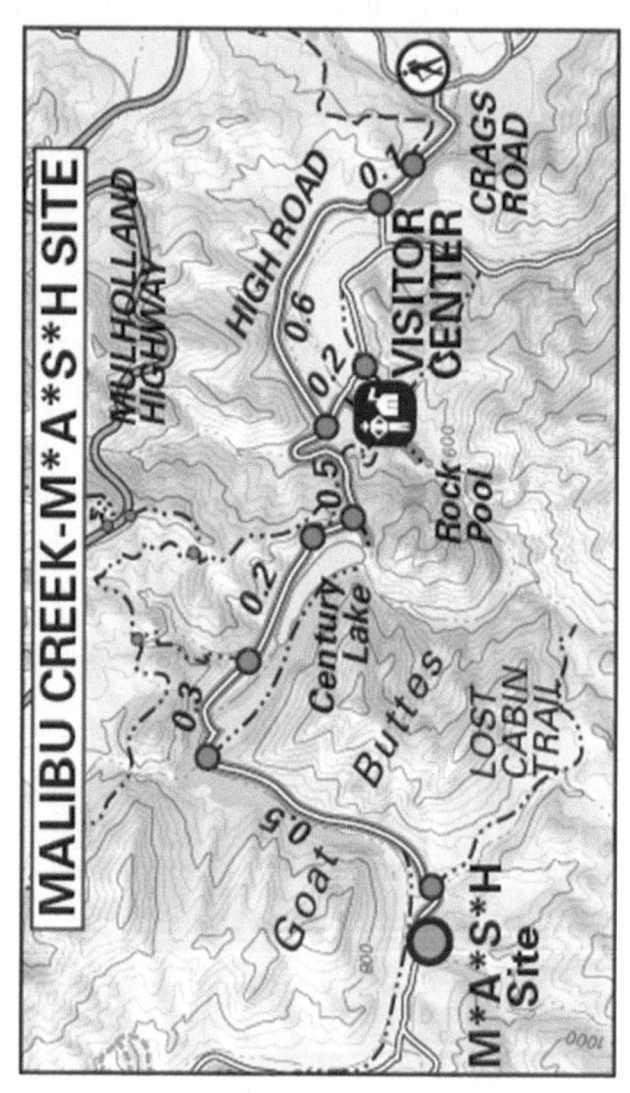

MALIBU CREEK

CRAGS ROAD, HIGH ROAD TRAILS

From Main Parking Area to Century Lake is 2.8 miles round trip with 100-foot elevation gain; to M*A*S*H site is 6 miles round trip with 200-foot gain

Before land for Malibu Creek State Park was acquired in 1974, it was divided into three parcels belonging to Bob Hope, Ronald Reagan and 20th Century Fox. Although the park is still used for moviemaking, it's primarily a haven for day hikers and picnickers.

Today the state park preserves more than 7,000 acres of rugged country in the middle of the Santa Monica Mountains.

The trail along Malibu Creek explores the heart of the state park. It's an easy, nearly level walk that visits a dramatic rock gorge, Century Lake and several locales popular with moviemakers.

Fans of the long-running TV show, M*A*S*H, will enjoy making the pilgrimage to the site where so many episodes were filmed. Some rusted vehicles, interpretive panels, a picnic table and helicopter pad are at the site. The prominent Goat Buttes that tower above Malibu Creek were featured in the opening shot of each episode.

DIRECTIONS: From Pacific Coast Highway, turn inland on Malibu Canyon Road and proceed 6.5 miles to the park entrance, 0.25 mile south of Mulholland Highway. If you're coming from the San Fernando Valley, exit the Ventura Freeway (101) on Las Virgenes Road and continue four miles to the park entrance.

THE HIKE: From the parking area, descend a staircase near the restrooms at the western edge of the parking lot. Cross a small bridge, passing signs marked "Backcountry Trails." Crags Road soon forks into a high road and a low road. Go right and walk along the oak-shaded high road, which makes a long, lazy left arc as it follows the north bank of Malibu Creek. You'll reach an intersection and turn left on a short road that crosses a bridge over Malibu Creek.

Gorge Trail is well worth a detour; follow it upstream a short distance to the gorge, one of the most dramatic sights in the Santa Monica Mountains. Malibu Creek makes a hairpin turn through 400-foot volcanic rock cliffs and cascades into aptly named Rock Pool. The Swiss Family Robinson television series and some Tarzan movies were filmed here, as were a number of scenes from the "Planet of the Apes" series of flicks.

Retrace your steps back to the high road and bear left toward Century Lake. As the road ascends you'll be treated to a fine view of Las Virgenes Valley. When you gain the crest of the hill, you'll look down on Century Lake. Near the lake are hills of porous lava and topsy-turvy sedimentary rock layers that tell of the violent geologic upheaval that formed Malibu Canyon. A side trail leads down to the lake which was scooped out by members of Crag's Country Club, a group of wealthy, turn-of-the-20th century businessmen who had a nearby lodge.

The road follows a (usually) dry creek bed though, after a good rain, it can be wet and wild going. Soon after passing a junction with the Lost Cabin Trail, you'll reach the M*A*S*H site.

Lovely Malibu Creek (pre-fire), flowing free.

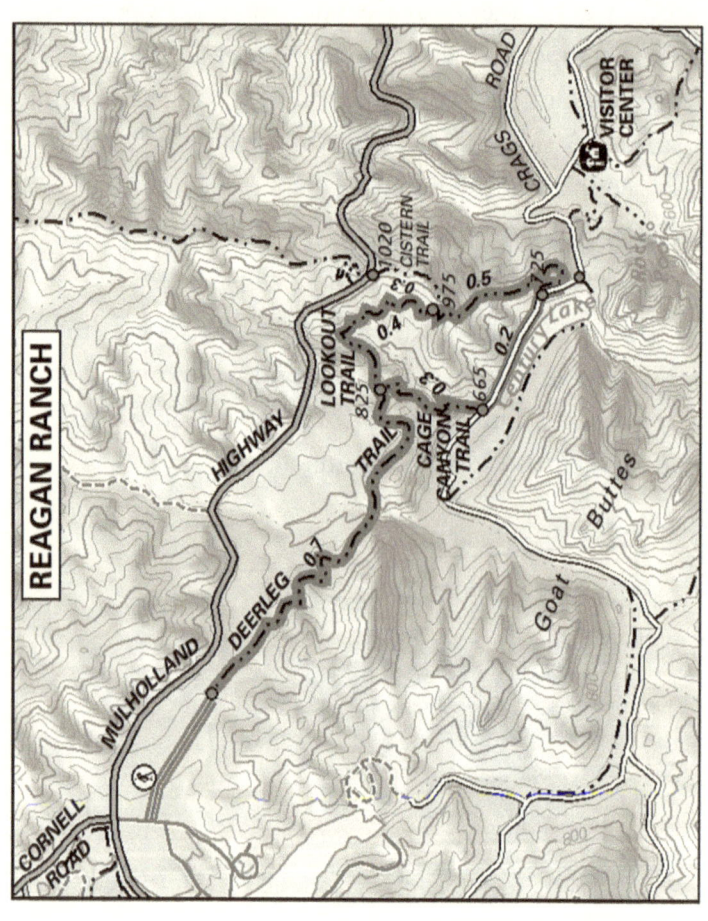

Reagan Ranch

Deerleg, Lookout, Cage Canyon Trails

3.4-mile loop through Malibu Creek State Park

Before plunging into the world of politics, actor Ronald Reagan owned a ranch in the Santa Monica Mountains. Reagan's Ranch, now part of Malibu Creek State Park, is a delight for hikers, who can enjoy the ranch's rolling meadowland and grand old oaks, and even probe the origins of the president's conservative political philosophy.

During the 1950s when Reagan hosted television's "Death Valley Days," he desired a more rural retreat than his home in Pacific Palisades. He bought the 305-acre ranch in the hills of Malibu as a place to raise thoroughbred horses. Land rose greatly in value, and taxes likewise; the tax increases really piqued Reagan and influenced his political philosophy. From this point on, he would be hostile toward government programs that required more and more tax dollars to fund.

When Reagan was elected governor in 1966, he moved to Sacramento and sold his ranch to a movie company. Today the ranch makes up the northwest corner of Malibu Creek State Park. The Reagan barn still stands and is now used for offices and storage by state park employees.

Trails loop through the Reagan Ranch and connect with the main part of the state park. My favorite hike uses a combo of short trails to explore Reagan Country.

DIRECTIONS: From Santa Monica, take Pacific Coast Highway up-coast to Malibu Canyon Road, turn inland and proceed to Mulholland Highway. Turn left and drive 3 miles to the ranch entrance at the corner of Mulholland and Cornell Road.

Or from the Ventura Freeway (101) in Agoura, exit on Kanan Road and head south. Make a left on Cornell Road and follow it to its intersection with Mulholland Highway. Park in the lot off Cornell Road.

THE HIKE: Walk the paved, then dirt, park road (Yearling Road). The trail leads past a row of stately eucalyptus and the old Reagan barn to the trailhead. Join Deer Leg Trail, which meanders past large oaks and crosses Udell Creek.

North of the trail and parallel to it, is a more informal pathway, Yearling Trail. The meadow here is a delight to behold in spring when lupine, larkspur and poppies pop out all over.

At the east end of the meadow, about a mile from the trailhead, you'll come to a three-way junction. Cage Canyon Trail forks right, but you'll head east on Lookout Trail, which tunnels through chaparral and ascends an oak crowned ridge to a junction with Cistern Trail, a short connector that leads north to Mulholland. Atop the ridge is a great view of Malibu Creek and the main features of the state park.

From the ridge, Lookout Trail drops a half mile to Crags Road, the state park's major trail, near Century Lake. Bear right, northwest for 0.2 mile to meet signed Cage Canyon Trail on your right.

Cage Canyon Trail makes a short (0.3 mile) and rapid ascent of the oak- and sycamore-filled canyon to Deer Leg Trail. Here you bear left and retrace your steps a mile back to the trailhead.

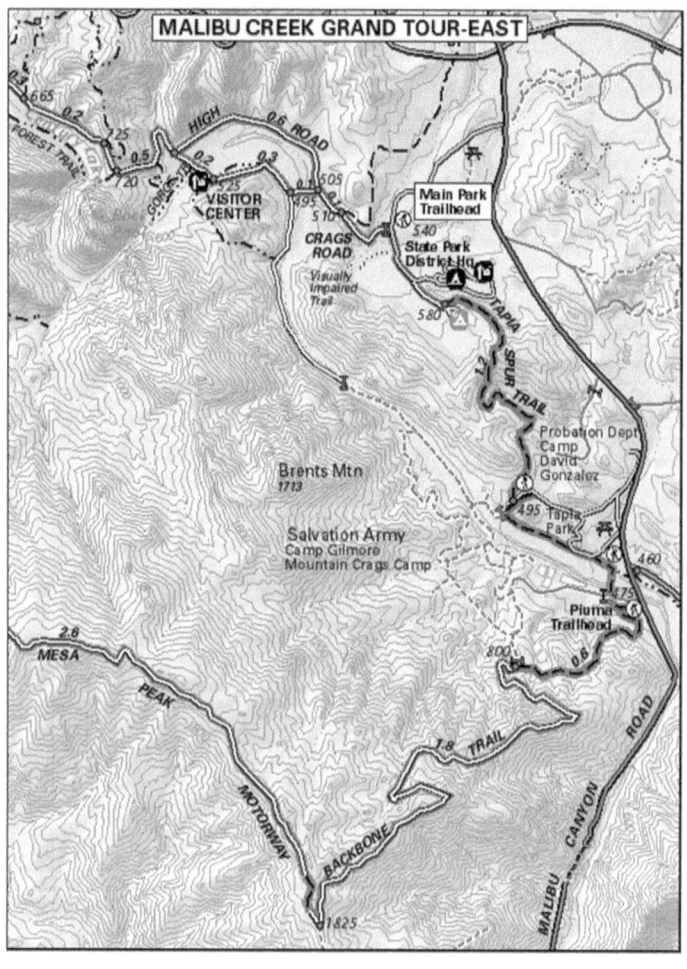

TheTrailmaster.com

MALIBU CREEK STATE PARK GRAND TOUR

BACKBONE TRAIL

From main parking lot to Castro Crest is 7 miles one way with 2,000 foot gain; return via Bulldog Motorway and Crags Road is 14 miles round trip

The Backbone Trail route through Malibu Creek State Park is one of the highlights of the 65-mile trail that extends across the spine of the Santa Monica Mountains. Combine this ridge-running trail with a loop back through the main part of the park for a memorable tour.

Get ocean and island views along the first half of the hike and explore geologically and ecologically unique Malibu Creek Canyon on the return leg. Some hikers like to start the grand tour at the Piuma Trailhead just south of the state park.

DIRECTIONS: From Pacific Coast Highway, turn inland on Malibu Canyon Road and proceed 6.5

miles to the park entrance, 0.25 mile south of Mulholland Highway. From the San Fernando Valley side of the mountains, exit the Ventura Freeway (101) on Las Virgenes Road and continue 4 miles to the park entrance.

THE HIKE: Follow a dirt road that skirts this parking area, leads past a giant valley oak and approaches the state park's campground. Bear right on a dirt road that leads a short distance through meadowland to the park's Group Camp. Here you'll join a 1.2-mile long connector trail, Tapia Spur Trail, that leads up and over a brushy ridge to the private Salvation Army Camp and into oak-shaded Tapia Park, once a county park and now a unit of Malibu Creek State Park.

The trail leads to a signed junction near a restroom and close to the Backbone Trail's Piuma Trailhead parking area by Malibu Canyon Road. Join the signed Backbone Trail, a footpath, on a 0.6 mile ascent southwest to meet a wider fire road. Now it climbs in earnest to the spine of the range at around 1,800 feet.

Enjoy sweeping panoramic views of Point Dume, Santa Monica Bay, and Palos Verdes Peninsula. On clear days, Catalina, Anacapa and Santa Cruz islands float upon the horizon.

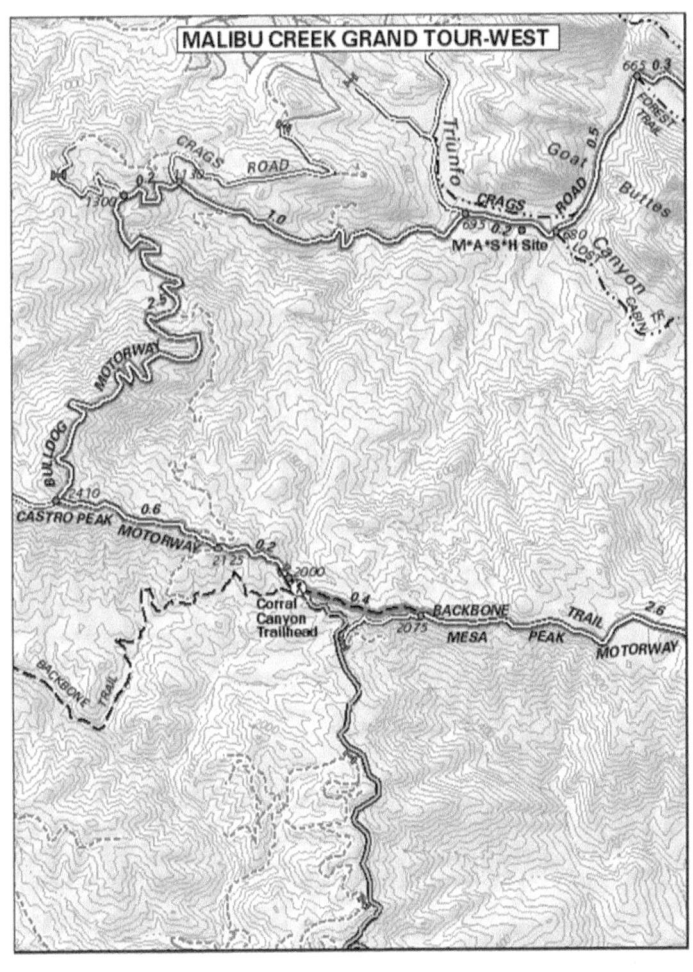

The trail veers left (south) toward Mesa Peak (1,844 feet) and a junction with Mesa Peak Motorway (a.k.a. Backbone Trail). You'll angle right at this junction and continue climbing in a northwesterly direction through an area rich in fossilized shells. Hillside roadcuts betray the Santa Monica Mountains' oceanic heritage. As you hike the spine of the range, a good view to the north is yours: the volcanic rocks of Goat Butte tower above Malibu Creek gorge and the path of Triunfo Canyon can be traced.

The road passes through an area of interesting sandstone formations, too. About 2.6 miles from the Mesa Peak Junction, the fire road gives way to a right-branching footpath that leads another 0.4 mile west to the Corral Canyon Road parking area. Here you leave the Backbone Trail and join clearly signed Castro Peak Motorway, a dirt road. Continue west on a mild ascent for 0.8 mile, reaching the signed intersection with Bulldog Motorway.

Congratulate yourself that you've accomplished more than half of the hike (7.7 miles) and by far the harder half. Bear right on Bulldog Motorway. Descend steeply under electrical transmission lines. (The first mile, which descends past some intriguing sandstone outcroppings, is especially steep.)

Some 2.7 miles of descent brings you to a junction with Crags Road, where you'll turn right (east) dropping into Triunfo Canyon and reaching the location of the exterior sets used by the M*A*S*H TV series. (The set is now on display in the Smithsonian.) The prominent Goat Buttes that tower above Malibu Creek are featured in the opening shot of each episode.

The road passes Century Lake, crosses a ridge, then drops down to Malibu Creek and comes to a fork in the road. Take either the left (high road) or continue straight ahead over the bridge on the low road and past the visitor center; the roads meet again downstream, so you may select either one. When the roads rejoin, follow Crags to the park's day use parking area.

*Hike along Malibu Creek to the former M*A*S*H TV series site, perhaps the most famed film location in the mountains.*

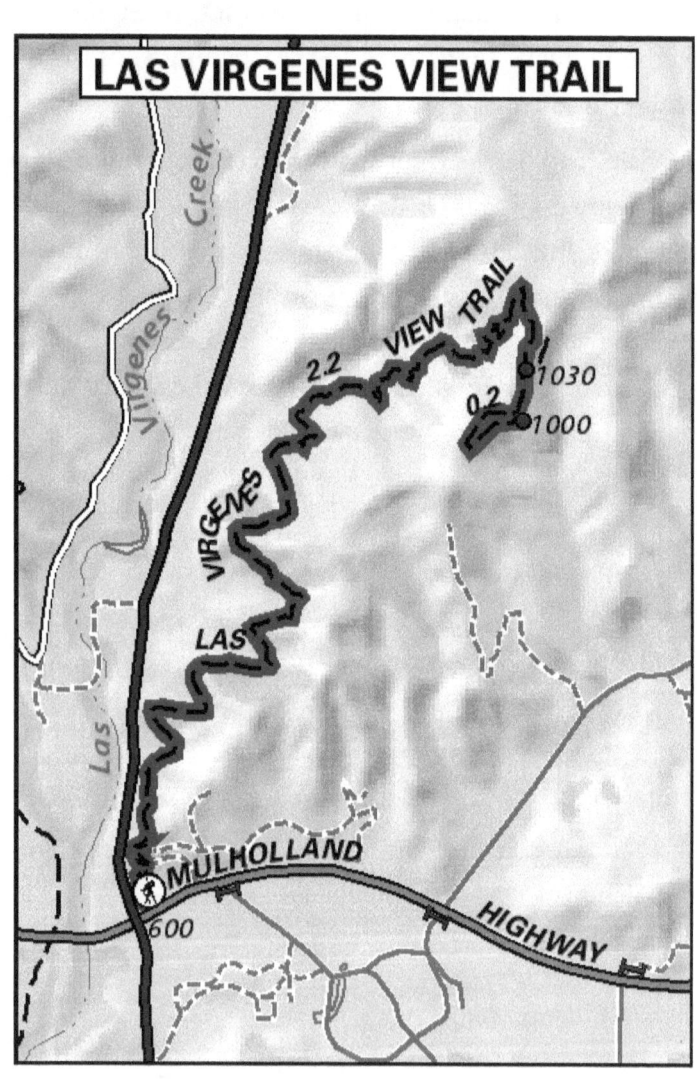

Las Virgenes View Park

Las Virgenes View Trail

From Mulholland Drive to Vista Point is 4.8 miles round trip with 500-foot elevation gain

For good vistas of the central portion of the Santa Monica Mountains, ascend Las Virgenes View Trail. The path traverses the similarly named Las Virgenes View Park, located just a stone's throw east of famed Malibu Creek State Park.

This is one of the fine "Single Trail Parks" in the Santa Monica Mountains. The hiker's reward for the short but sweet ascent to the 1,100-foot top of the trail is a 360-degree panorama of the eastern and central parts of the range, as well as Malibu Canyon and surrounding communities.

On my hikes I've observed a surprising number of animals along this trail: a western fence lizard basking on a sunny rock, a red-tailed hawk soaring over the grasslands, mule deer browsing the brush, an acorn woodpecker rat-a-tat-tatting against a tree trunk, a coyote jogging along a high ridge. What seemed to me so incongruous about this wildlife drama is that it plays out within sight of the Ventura Freeway.

Cattle used to graze Las Virgenes View Park and the private property surrounding it. The first time I hiked across the park a black and white bovine blocked a narrow part of the path for some time while we negotiated who would continue along the trail and who would climb off-trail into the brush. (The heaviest, most patient animal, the one with the horns, prevailed in this standoff.)

The 696-acre park preserves several of the major plant communities common to the Santa Monica Mountains, including chaparral, oak woodland, and a riparian zone highlighted by sycamore, black cottonwood, willow and bay. A rare valley grassland contains purple needle grass and blue-eye grass, two native species that managed to survive two centuries of cattle grazing.

DIRECTIONS: From the Ventura Freeway (101) in Calabasas, exit on Las Virgenes Road. Head south 3 miles to a stop-lighted intersection with Mulholland Highway. Las Virgenes View Trail begins at the northeast corner of the intersection, where there's limited parking. More parking is available at the southwestern corner, on the border of Malibu Creek State Park.

Use caution at this intersection. Traffic moves at very high speeds in all directions.

THE HIKE: Las Virgenes View Trail ascends north on a more or less parallel course to Las Virgenes Road. Contemplate the scene from a trailside bench located a quarter-mile out. After another half mile, an intriguing section of trail wanders across a narrow ledge.

As the path twists and turns, civilization's cacophony recedes, though views of that civilization—Calabasas, the Ventura Freeway and more—actually get more distinct. Reaching a ridgeline, the trail bends south along a wire fence. On hot days you'll appreciate the shade offered en route by the scattered oaks.

Enjoy the stirring views, which include Castro Peak and Goat Buttes in Malibu Creek State Park and Saddle Peak to the southeast. The trail makes a tight loop atop the ridgeline and you return the way you came.

Newton Canyon Falls
Backbone Trail

From Kanan-Dume Road to Newton Canyon Falls is 1 mile round trip

Ferns, wildflowers and a year-round waterfall are among the wonders of Newton Canyon.

Reaching the 30-foot cascade is easy thanks to a convenient trailhead on Kanan Dume Road and short trail that travels the floor of the canyon amidst a tangle of bay laurel, oak and sycamore..

DIRECTIONS: From the Ventura Freeway (101) in Agoura Hills, exit on Kanan Road and proceed 7.6 miles south. The parking lot is located on the right side of the road immediately before entering the third tunnel along the road (Tunnel 1).

THE HIKE: From the signed trailhead, hike west on Backbone Trail, descending into the lush canyon. After crossing a side creek, join an unsigned path on the left. Look down at the top of the falls from a rock outcropping, then descend steeply to the canyon bottom.

Hike up-creek and soon spot Newton Canyon Falls spilling into a handsome mossy grotto.

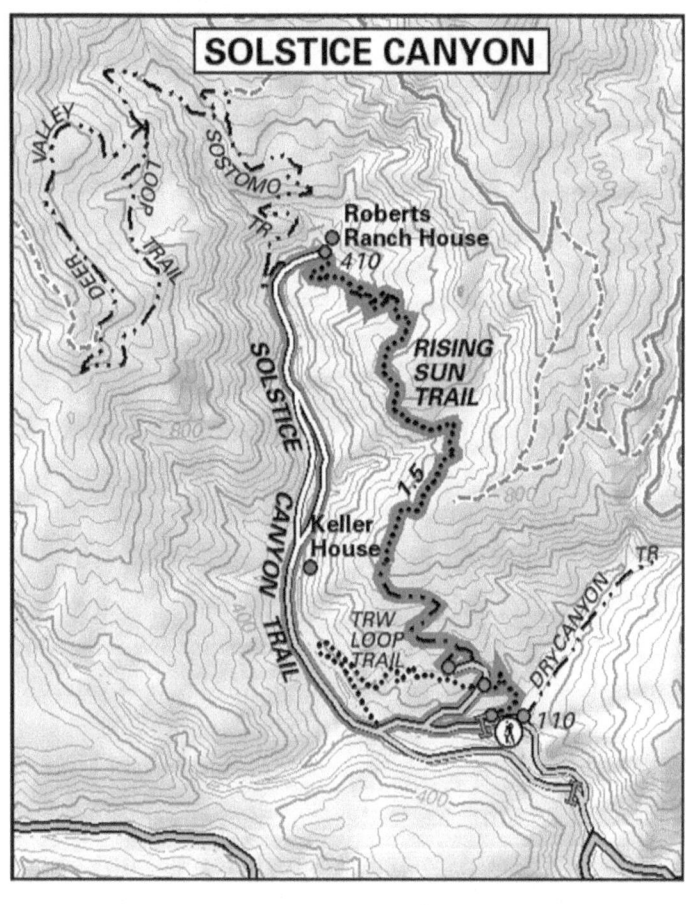

TheTrailmaster.com

Solstice Canyon Park

Solstice Canyon, Rising Sun Trails

To waterfall and Roberts Ranch house ruins is 3 miles round trip with 400-foot elevation gain

At least some of the serenity and scenery offered by Solstice Canyon has returned. The 2007 Corral Fire scorched the canyon's hillsides and thereafter vast amounts of soil and rock debris were later dislodged and fell into the canyon.

However, some of the chaparral plants and grasses quickly re-colonized and Solstice Canyon is once more becoming a favorite of hikers.

Several historic buildings were lost in the fire, including the 1865 Mathew Keller House. The fire damaged Solstice Canyon's strangest structure sometimes compared to a futurist farm house with a silo attached. From 1961 to 1973 Space Tech Labs, a subsidiary of TRW used the building to conduct tests to determine the magnetic sensitivity of satellite instrumentation.

Solstice Canyon Park opened on summer solstice, 1988. The Santa Monica Mountains Conservancy purchased the land from the Roberts family and transformed the 550-acre Roberts Ranch into a park. Today National Park Service rangers are the stewards of Solstice Canyon.

NPS officials are working to regenerate native plant species lost in the blaze and attempting to prevent invasive non-native species from returning to an area with a long history of human presence. Hikers will observe much progress toward the habitat restoration of Solstice Canyon.

The main canyon path is a narrow country road—suitable for strollers and wheelchairs—and offers an easy family hike in the shade of grand old oaks and towering sycamores. In autumn, enjoy the fall color display of the sycamores and in winter, from the park's upper slopes, look for gray whales migrating past Point Dume.

DIRECTIONS: From Pacific Coast Highway, about 17 miles up-coast from Santa Monica and 3.5 miles up-coast from Malibu Canyon Road, turn inland on Corral Canyon Road. At the first bend in the road, you'll leave the road and proceed straight to the parking lot, where there are restrooms and a shelter used for educational programs.

THE HIKE: Walk up the wide road. About halfway along, you'll pass what's left of the 1865 Mathew Keller House and in a few more minutes—Fern Grotto. The road travels under the shade of oak and sycamore to its end at the remains of the old Roberts Ranch House.

Palms, agave, bamboo, bird of paradise and many more tropical plants once thrived in the Roberts' family garden gone wild.

A waterfall, fountain and an old dam were some of the other special features found in this paradisiacal setting known as Tropical Terrace. It's no paradise these days, but the waterfall still tumbles with sufficient rainfall.

Across the creek from Tropical Terrace is signed Rising Sun Trail, which climbs a ridge for rewarding canyon and ocean views. The two-mile trail offers an excellent, but more difficult, return route to the trailhead.

A rocky window offers a great look at the wild west end of the Santa Monica Mountains.

EVERY TRAIL TELLS A STORY.

Santa Monica Mountains

West

HIKE ON.

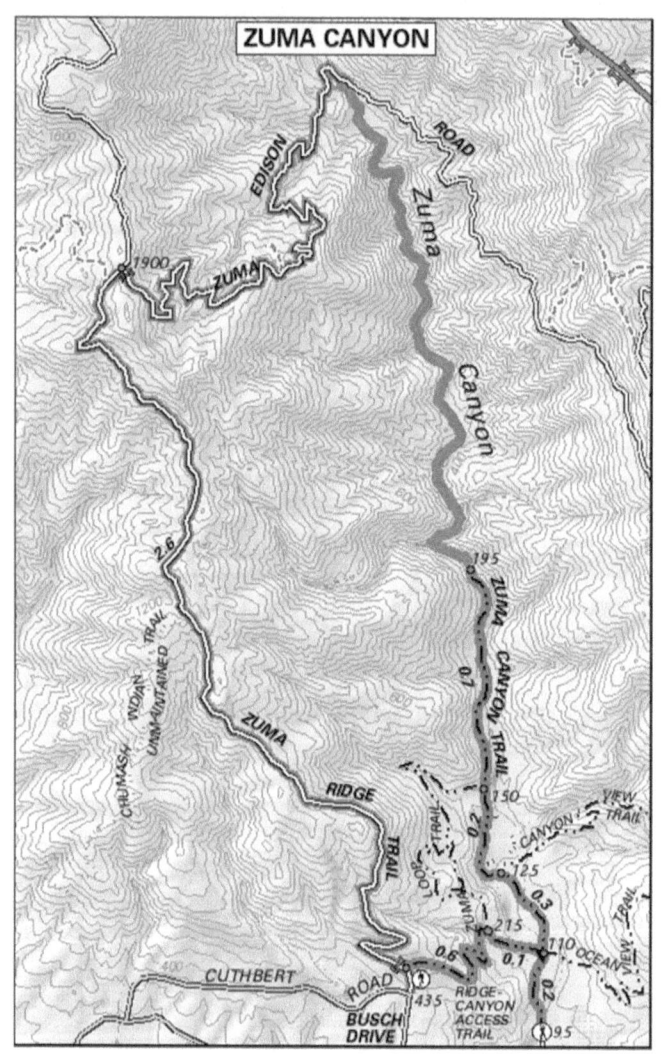

ZUMA CANYON

ZUMA CANYON TRAIL

To trail's end is 3 miles round trip with 100-foot elevation gain; to Zuma-Edison Road is 6.8 miles round trip with 600-foot gain; return via Zuma Ridge Trail is 8.2-mile loop with 1,800-foot gain

Zuma Canyon is a living illustration of the Santa Monica Mountains of a century ago: a creek cascading over magnificent sandstone boulders, a jungle of willow and lush streamside flora, fern-fringed pools and towering rock walls.

The canyon is one of the gems of the Santa Monica Mountains. National Park Service staff improved trails, but wisely left well enough alone, preserving the wild and remote flavor of this rugged country.

Partake of Zuma Canyon's grandeur with a mellow walk to the end of the trail and by two miles of trail-less creek-crossing and boulder-hopping—one of the most challenging hikes in the Santa Monicas.

Return via Zuma Ridge Trail and enjoy grand ocean and mountain views.

Looking for an easier hike? Combine Ocean View and Canyon View trails for a great introduction to the charms of lower Zuma Canyon. Both trails forming a 3.1-mile loop (with 600-foot elevation gain) are true to their names, with the added bonus of Ocean View Trail also offering canyon views and Canyon View Trail also offering ocean views.

In winter, the canyon can be inaccessible because of high water levels. In spring, the lovely creek is energetic, but crossings manageable. In summer—well, it's not the heat it's the humidity; the canyon's tight confines and jungle-like vegetation combine to make uncomfortable hiking. Autumn months are great for hiking because the creek is low and the weather mild.

DIRECTIONS: From Pacific Coast Highway in Malibu, head up-coast one mile past an intersection with Kanan-Dume Road and turn right on Bonsall Drive (this turn is just before the turnoff for Zuma Beach). Drive a mile to road's end at a parking lot.

THE HIKE: From the parking area, head north on the main trail 0.2 mile to a three-way junction. Continue past junctions with Canyon View Trail and Ocean View Trail north into Zuma Canyon.

Nearly a mile from the trailhead, the canyon narrows and a half mile later the trail peters out in a cluster of boulders. Should you decide to continue up-canyon, boulders will be very much in your picture. Expect to boulder-hop small and mid-sized boulders and navigate around compact car and mid-size truck-sized boulders.

Also expect slow progress—one mile an hour or less. The only intrusions into the wilderness scene are sky-high powerlines over the canyon, about three miles from the trailhead, and Zuma-Edison Road that crosses the canyon another mile north.

Turn left on this road and ascend very steeply, gaining a thousand feet in elevation in less than a mile and an half by the time you reach Zuma Ridge Trail (a fire road). Turn left (south).

Enjoy the coastal and mountain views as you descend rapidly on this popular mountain bike route, dropping 1,500 feet in elevation over the course of 2.6 miles to the Busch Drive Trailhead and parking area. Here you'll join the signed trail and travel east 0.6 miles to the main trail network for Zuma Canyon and then another 0.3 mile back to where you began this hike.

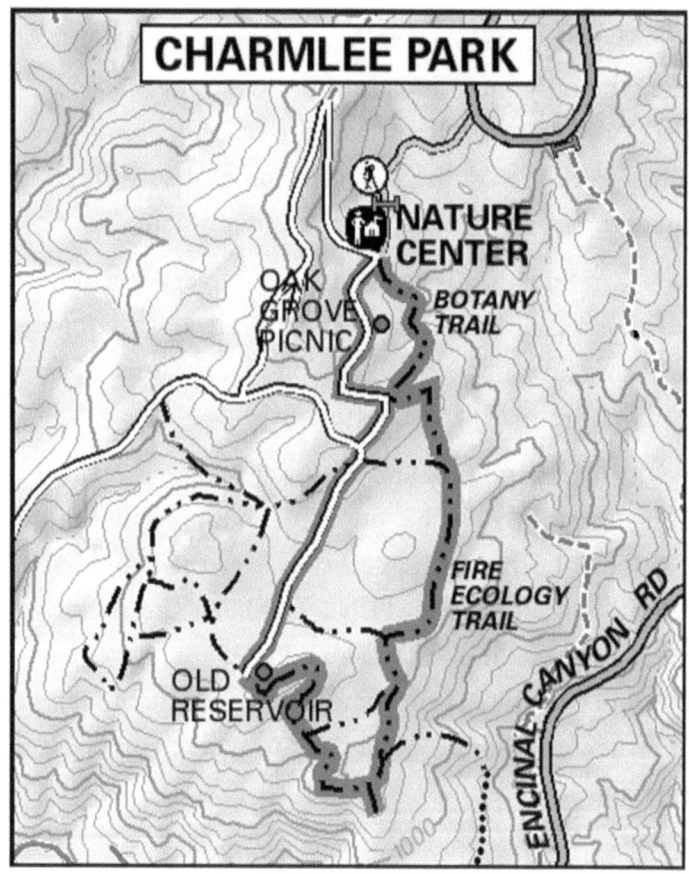

Charmlee Wilderness Park

Meadow Ranch, Fire Ecology, Botany Trails

2-mile loop around the park

Charmlee, perched on the blufftops above Malibu, often has outstanding spring wildflower displays. Most of the park is a large open meadow; the flower display, given timely rainfall, can be quite colorful. Lupine, paintbrush, larkspur, mariposa lily, penstemon and California peony bust out all over.

Stop at Charmlee's small nature center and inquire about what's blooming where. Also pick up a copy of a brochure that interprets the park's Fire Ecology Trail. This nature trail interprets the important role of fire in Southern California's chaparral communities.

Good views are another reason to visit Charmlee, operated by the City of Malibu Department of Parks and Recreation. The Santa Monica Mountains spread east to west, with the Simi Hills and Santa Susana

Mountains rising to the north. Down-coast you can see Zuma Beach and Point Dume and up-coast Sequit Point in Leo Carrillo State Park.

Beginning in the early 1800s, this Malibu meadowland was part of Rancho Topanga-Malibu-Sequit and was used to pasture cattle. For a century and a half, various ranchers held the property. Last of these private landholders—Charmain and Leonard Swartz—combined their first names to give Charmlee its euphonious name.

For the hiker, 530-acre Charmlee is one of the few parks, perhaps the only park, offering a surplus of trails. Quite a few paths and old ranch roads—nine miles worth no less—wind through the park, which is shaped like a big grassy bowl.

Because the park is mostly one big meadow fringed with oak trees, it's easy to see where you're going and improvise your own circle tour of Charmlee.

DIRECTIONS: From Pacific Coast Highway, about 12 miles up-coast from the community of Malibu, take Encinal Canyon Road 4.5 miles to Charmlee Wilderness Park.

THE HIKE: From the parking lot, walk past the restrooms, and visit the native plant garden. Next stroll through the park's Oak Grove Picnic Area on a dirt road. Travel under the shade of coast live oaks on the road, which crests a low rise, offers a couple of side trails to the left to explore, and soon arrives at a more distinct junction with a fire road leading downhill along the eastern edge of the meadow. This is a good route to take because it leads to fine ocean views.

Take this to the Old Reservoir, then travel downcoast along the tall bluffs to a couple of ocean overlooks, including one rocky outcropping that offers particularly terrific views. Circle back inland by a trail leading toward an oak grove, one of the park's many picturesque picnic spots.

Join Fire Ecology Trail for a close-up look at how Southern California's Mediterranean flora has adapted to fire and aptly named Botany Trail to loop back to Oak Grove Picnic Area and the trailhead.

Flowers everywhere, including caterpillar phacelia, at Charmlee Park

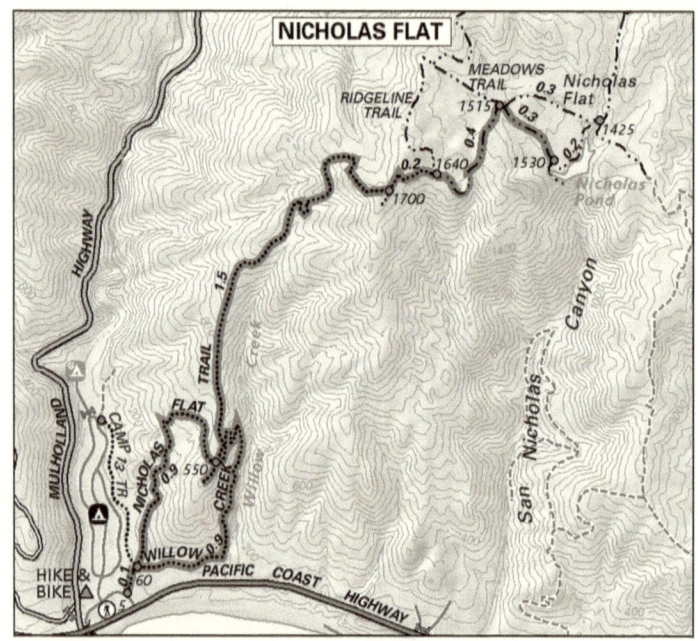

NICHOLAS FLAT

NICHOLAS FLAT TRAIL

From Leo Carrillo State Park entry road to Nicholas Flat is 6.6 miles round trip with 1,600-foot elevation gain

Leo Carrillo State Park's Nicholas Flat area is one of the best spots in the Santa Monica Mountains for spring wildflowers because it's a meeting place for four plant communities: chaparral, grassland, coastal scrub and oak woodland.

Another reason for the remarkable plant diversity is the park's elevation, which varies from sea level to nearly 2,000 feet. Along park trails, look for shooting star, hedge nettle, sugar bush, purple sage, chamise, blue dick, deer weed, burr clover, bush lupine, golden yarrow, fuschia-flowered gooseberry, and many more flowering plants.

Nicholas Flat's charms also include a big meadow, a pond, and Malibu coast views.

DIRECTIONS: From the west end of the Santa Monica Freeway in Santa Monica, head up-coast on

Pacific Coast Highway about 25 miles to Leo Carrillo State Beach. There's free parking along Coast Highway, and fee parking in the park's day use area.

THE HIKE: Locate the trailhead a short distance past the park entry kiosk, opposite the day use parking area. Join signed Camp 13 Trail, which almost immediately splits. The right branch (Willow Creek Trail) circles the hill, climbs above Willow Creek, and after a mile, rejoins the main Nicholas Flat Trail. Enjoy this interesting option on your return from Nicholas Flat.

Take the left branch, which immediately begins a moderate to steep ascent of the grassy slopes above the park campground. The trail switchbacks through a coastal scrub community up to a saddle on the ridgeline. Here you'll meet Willow Creek, the alternate branch of Nicholas Flat Trail. From the saddle, a

Peaceful Nicholas Pond, prettier than a picture

short side trail leads south to a hilltop, where there's a fine coastal view. From the viewpoint, observe Point Dume and the Malibu coastline.

Following the ridgeline, Nicholas Flat Trail climbs inland over a chaparral-covered slope. Enjoy increasingly grand coastal views and survey the open slopes, browsed by nimble deer.

After a good deal of climbing, the trail levels atop the ridgeline and, about 2.6 miles from the trailhead, intersects Ridgeline Trail coming in from the north. Keep right and continue another 0.4 mile to another junction, a four-way. Meadows Trail heads west while two trails head east 0.3 mile to Nicholas Pond—one to the north end of the pond, and one to the south end. (A 0.2-mile long trail leads along the pond shore and connects the two trails.)

Picnic beneath the shady oaks or in the meadow. The man-made pond is backed by handsome boulders. From the south end of the pond, a sketchy path leads up to a rocky perch that offers commanding coastal views.

Return the way you came until reaching the junction located 0.9 mile from the trailhead. Bear left at the fork and hike Willow Creek Trail as it descends into the canyon cut by Willow Creek, contours around an ocean-facing slope, and returns you to the trailhead.

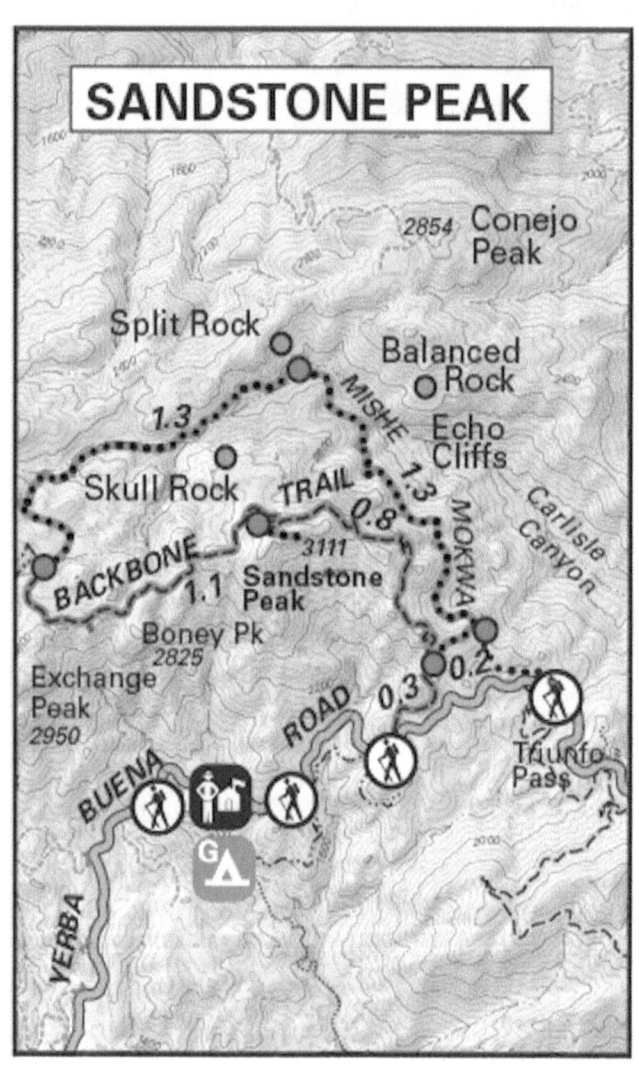

Sandstone Peak

Backbone Trail, Mishe Mokwa Trail

6 miles round trip with 900-foot elevation gain.

Sandstone Peak, highest peak in the Santa Monica Mountains, is one of the highlights of a visit to Circle X Ranch, 1,655 acres of National Park Service land on the border of Los Angeles and Ventura counties. The parkland boasts more than 30 miles of trail.

The ranch once belonged to movie actor Donald Crisp, who starred in "How Green was My Valley." The Exchange Club purchased the nucleus of the park in 1949 and gave it to the Boy Scouts. The emblem for the Exchange Club was a circled X—hence the name of the ranch.

Sandstone Peak offers outstanding views from its 3,111-foot summit, though "Sandstone" is certainly a misnomer; the peak is a large mass of volcanic rock.

DIRECTIONS: Drive up-coast on Pacific Coast Highway past Malibu, a mile past the Los Angeles

County line. Turn inland on Yerba Buena Road and proceed five miles to Circle X Ranch. Pass the park's headquarters building and continue one more mile to the signed trailhead on your left and plenty of parking.

THE HIKE: From the signed trailhead, walk up the fire road 0.3 mile to a signed junction with Mishe Mokwa Trail. Leave the fire road here and join the trail, which climbs and contours over the brushy slopes of Boney Mountain.

Breaks in the brush offer good views to the right of historic Triunfo Pass, used by the Chumash to travel from inland to the coast. Mishe Mokwa Trail levels and tunnels through chaparral.

The path then descends into Carlisle Canyon. Across the canyon are striking red volcanic formations, among them well-named Balanced Rock. The path, shaded by oak and laurel, drops into the canyon at another aptly-named rock formation—Split Rock, 1.8 miles from the trailhead. Here you'll find a picnic area, shaded by oak and sycamore. An all-year creek and a spring add to the site's charm.

From Split Rock, ascend out of Carlisle Canyon. From the road's high point, look straight-ahead up at a pyramid-like volcanic rock formation known as Egyptian Rock.

About 1.3 miles from Split Rock, Mishe Mokwa Trail meets the Backbone Trail. West fork of the trail leads toward Point Mugu State Park, but you head south and before long bend east on the fire road.

Look sharply to the right for the short, unsigned spur trail to Inspiration Point. Mount Baldy and Catalina are among the inspiring sights pointed out by a geographical locator monument.

Keep climbing with the fire road. After a few switchbacks, look for a steep trail on the right. Follow this trail to the top of Sandstone Peak.

Enjoy commanding, clear-day views: the Topatopa Mountains, haunt of the condors, the Oxnard Plain, the Channel Islands, and the wide blue Pacific. After enjoying the view, return to the Backbone Trail (road) and descend a bit more than a mile back to the trailhead.

No doubt about it: Sandstone is the highest peak.

Rancho Sierra Vista

Sycamore Canyon Road, Satwiwa Loop Trail

To Sycamore Canyon Falls is 3 miles round trip with 300-foot elevation gain; return via Satwiwa Loop Trail is 4 miles round trip

Take a hike to Sycamore Canyon Falls, comprised of a half a dozen waterfalls cascading into pools bordered by handsome sandstone canyon walls. Oaks, sycamores, big-leaf maples, woodwardia and sword ferns grace the canyon bottom nearby.

Rancho Sierra Vista/Satwiwa, located on the north boundary of Point Mugu State Park, offers the opportunity explore a place where Chumash walked for thousands of years before Europeans arrived on the scene. A visitor center and guest speakers help moderns learn the habits of birds and animals, the changes the seasons bring, and gain insight into the ceremonies that kept—and still keep—the Chumash bonded to the earth.

For hunter-gatherers, as anthropologists call them, this land on the wild west end of the Santa Monica Mountains was truly bountiful: seeds, roots, bulbs, berries, acorns and black walnuts. Birds, deer and squirrel were plentiful, as were fish and shellfish from nearby Mugu Lagoon. This abundant food supply helped the Chumash become the largest tribal group in California.

The name of this park site, Rancho Sierra Vista/Satwiwa reflects its history as both a longtime (1870-1970) horse and cattle ranch and ancestral land of the Chumash. The National Park Service prefers to call Satwiwa a culture center rather than a museum to keep the emphasis on living Native Americans.

DIRECTIONS: From the Ventura Freeway (Highway 101) in Newbury Park, exit on Wendy Drive and head south a mile to Borchard Road. Turn right and travel 0.5 mile to Reino Road.

Turn left and proceed 1.2 miles to Lynn Road, turn right and continue another 1.2 miles to the park entrance road (Via Goleta) on the south side of the road.

The paved park road passes equestrian parking on the right and a small day use parking lot on the left before dead-ending at a large parking lot 0.7 miles from Lynn Road.

THE HIKE: From the parking lot, follow the wide service road 0.3 mile to signed Satwiwa Native American Indian Culture Center, then continue another 0.3 mile to the crest of a low ridge and the boundary with Point Mugu State Park. Gaze down at Big Sycamore Canyon, then go left (east) on Old Boney Trail.

Ascend briefly, pass a branch of Satwiwa Loop Trail and continue to a fork. Take the right fork, descending 0.4 mile to a junction with Upper Sycamore Canyon Trail, and continuing past this junction another 0.2 mile to a tight bend and the side trail on your left leading to Sycamore Canyon Falls. Hike along the creek, crossing it, and boulder-hopping to the falls, which spills into a quiet grotto.

Retrace your steps back to the Satwiwa Loop Trail and bend north to junction a connector trail leading to Wendy Drive, then west toward an old cattle pond, now a haven for waterfowl and wildlife and to a Chumash village exhibit. From Satwiwa Culture Center, retrace your steps 0.3 mile on the service road back to the trailhead.

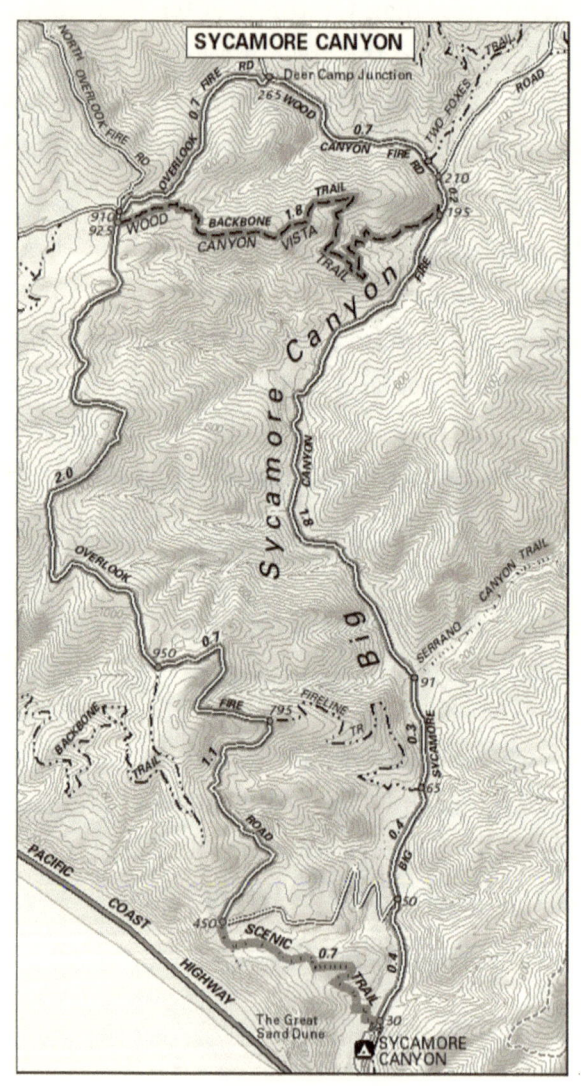

Sycamore Canyon

Sycamore Canyon Trail

From Big Sycamore Canyon to Deer Camp Junction is 7.6 miles round trip with 200-foot elevation gain; return via Overlook Trail is 9.7 miles round trip with 700-foot gain

Sycamore Canyon Trail takes you through a peaceful wooded canyon, where a multitude of monarch butterflies dwell in the fall, and past some magnificent sycamores. By some accounts, it's the finest example of a sycamore grove in the entire California State Parks system.

Or was. The 2013 Springs Fire ravaged Sycamore Canyon and some fine specimens were lost. All the trails leading through and from the canyon are open but know that nearly all the park was blackened by the blaze, and still recovering.

The trail follows the canyon on a gentle northern traverse across Point Mugu State Park, largest preserved area in the Santa Monica Mountains. This trail, combined with Overlook Trail, gives the hiker quite a tour of the park. The canyon offers flat, family-friendly outings as well.

DIRECTIONS: Drive up-coast on Highway 1, 32 miles from Santa Monica, to Big Sycamore Canyon Campground in Point Mugu State Park. Park in the day-use area (fee) or along Pacific Coast Highway (free). Walk through the campground to a locked yellow gate at the end of the campground loop and the trailhead for the Sycamore Canyon Fire Road.

THE HIKE: Take the trail up-canyon, following the creek. (Note Scenic Trail, leading westward; this could be an optional return route.) Winter rains cause the creek to rise, and sometimes keeping your feet dry while crossing is difficult. Underground water keeps much of the creekside vegetation green year-round.

About 0.4 from the campground, look for Overlook Trail, which switchbacks to the west up a ridge and then heads north toward the native tall grass prairie in La Jolla Valley. Make note of this trail, an optional return route.

Another 0.7 mile of nearly level canyon trail leads to a trail that branches right—Serrano Canyon Trail, an absolute gem. A mile more of easy walking beneath the sycamores brings you to an ideal picnic table shaded by a grove of large oak trees; this might be a good turnaround spot. Total round trip distance would be a bit more than 4 miles.

Continue up the canyon, pass beneath more giant sycamores, and soon arrive at a junction with the Backbone Trail, a.k.a. Wood Canyon Vista Trail. Join this path ascending west 1.8 miles to meet the Overlook Fire Road.

Or continue on Sycamore Canyon Trail another 0.2 mile and then bend northwest 0.7 mile to Deer Camp Junction, a fine lunch stop. Oaks predominate over sycamores along Wood Canyon Creek.

Call it a day here and return the way you came. Or return via Overlook Trail: Climb 0.7 mile on Overlook Fire Road to the divide between Sycamore Canyon and La Jolla Valley. Upon reaching a junction, head south on the Overlook Trail, staying on the La Jolla Canyon side of the ridge.

True to its name, Overlook Trail offers good views of grassy mountainsides, Boney Peak and Big Sycamore Canyon as it travels 3.8 miles to a junction with Scenic Trail. Take this trail, scenic and a shortcut, too, 0.7 mile southeast back to the trailhead.

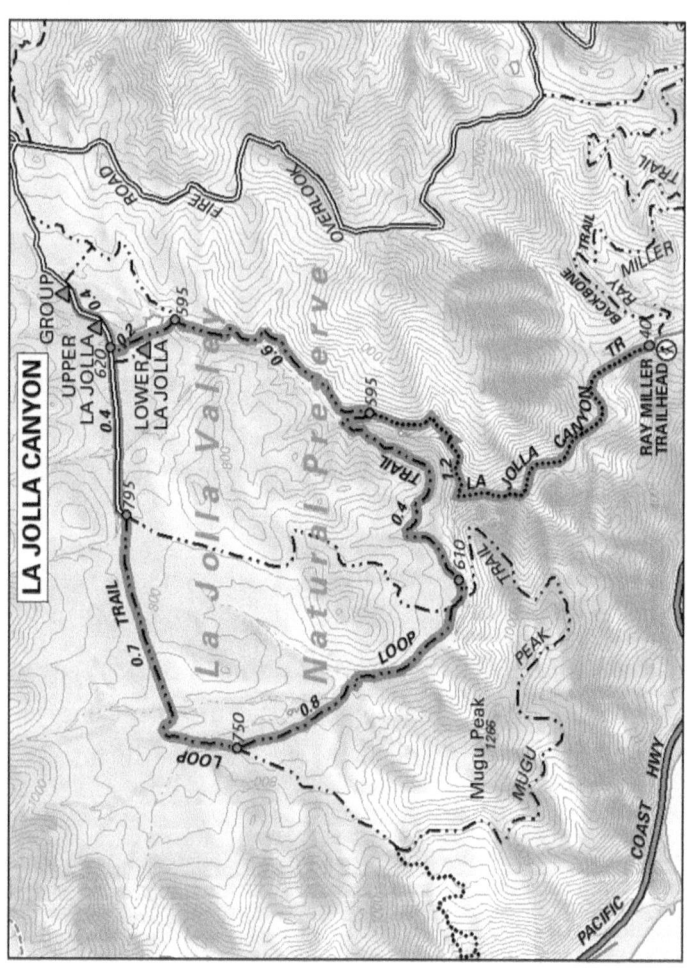

La Jolla Canyon

La Jolla Canyon, La Jolla Valley Loop Trails

From Ray Miller Trailhead to La Jolla Valley Camp is 4.8 miles round trip with 600-foot elevation gain; return via La Jolla Valley Loop Trail is 6 miles round trip with 700-foot gain

This hike explores two delights of Point Mugu State Park: La Jolla Canyon and La Jolla Valley Natural Preserve. Narrow and rugged La Jolla Canyon hosts a year-round creek, a waterfall and colonies of coreopsis, a.k.a. tree sunflower.

Ringed by ridges, the native grassland of La Jolla Valley welcomes the hiker with its drifts of oak and peaceful pond. This pastoral upland in the heart of park is a native grassland.

During the spring when wildflowers and coastal shrubs are in bloom, canyon and valley trails smell as good as they look. The trailhead, complete with restrooms, drinking water and picnic tables, honors volunteer ranger Ray Miller, first official camp host in the state park system.

DIRECTIONS: Drive about 30 miles up-coast on Pacific Coast Highway (1) from Santa Monica (21 miles up from Malibu Canyon Road if you're coming from the Ventura Freeway (101) and the San Fernando Valley). The turnoff is 1.5 miles north of Big Sycamore Canyon Trailhead, also part of Point Mugu State Park. The signed trailhead is located near an interpretive display, where the fire road leads into the canyon.

THE HIKE: From the yellow gate, the fire road leads north up the canyon along the creek.

The route crosses and re-crosses the creek and crosses again at the 0.8-mile mark just below a handsome 15-foot waterfall that tumbles down a natural rock staircase.

Past the falls, the trail passes giant coreopsis plants. Springtime travel on this trail takes the hiker past the blue and white blossoms of the ceanothus, black sage with its light-blue flowers (and pungent aroma!) and hummingbird sage with its crimson flowers.

At the first trail junction, with La Jolla Valley Loop Trail, stick with La Jolla Canyon Trail. In 0.6 mile, you'll arrive at another junction. Leave the main trail and explore a lovely cattail pond, nesting place for birds, including the redwing blackbird. Ducks and coots paddle the perimeter.

Continue on La Jolla Canyon Trail, skirt the east end of La Jolla Valley, enjoy an overview of waving grasses and intersect a "T" junction. Bear right at the fire road and walk a few minutes east to La Jolla Valley Camp. Campsites, sheltered by oaks and equipped with tables, are ideal picnic spots. For more picnicking, continue along the fire road to La Jolla Valley Group Camp.

Head back west on the fire road (La Jolla Valley Loop Trail), which climbs slightly to the hike's high point, passes a trail junction, levels, then bends south as it crosses the La Jolla Valley grasslands. Watch for deer and the rare and elusive chocolate lily.

Curving east, the loop trail passes a junction with Mugu Peak Trail, then travels a ridge northeast 0.4 mile to meet La Jolla Canyon Trail. Retrace your steps on this path 1.2 miles back to Ray Miller Trailhead.

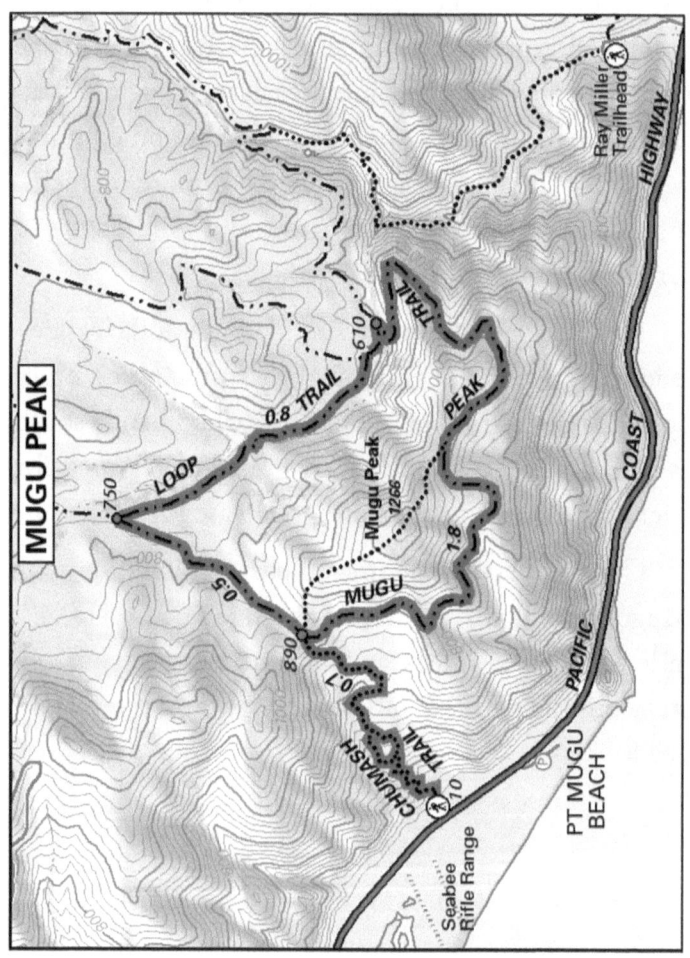

Mugu Peak

Chumash, Mugu Peak Trails

To Mugu Peak is 3 miles round trip with 1,250-foot elevation gain; loop via La Jolla Valley is 4.5 miles round trip

Mugu Peak anchors the wild west end of the Santa Monica Mountains. From the summit, the hiker gains grand mountain, ocean and island views. Ascending the peak, though, is quite the aerobic workout!

At the base of Mugu Peak lies La Jolla Valley, ringed by ridges and home to a native grassland, a rarity in Southern California. In taking a circle tour around the peak, you gaze over ocean waves, as well as waves of grass.

Super-steep Chumash Trail aggressively tackles a coastal slope dotted with cactus, yucca and yellow coreopsis, the so-called tree sunflower. Make a bee-line for Mugu Peak if you wish, but I prefer rounding the peak by trail and enjoying the natural attractions before heading up the peak for the panoramic views.

The 2013 Springs Fire burned 12,000 of the 14,000 acres of Point Mugu State Park and a majority of the park's 70 miles of trail.

DIRECTIONS: Head up-coast on Pacific Coast Highway some 35 miles from Santa Monica and about 3.5 miles past the Sycamore Canyon entrance to Point Mugu State Park. On the ocean side you'll spot Mugu Lagoon and the Seabee Rifle Range for the Point Mugu Naval Base and on the inland side a parking lot and signed Chumash Trail.

Warning: rangers report a more-than-usual amount of vehicle break-ins at this trailhead.

THE HIKE: Chumash Trail ascends relentlessly up the coastal scrub- and cactus-dotted slopes. Look behind you to mark your progress and to behold grand ocean views.

After 0.7 mile and a 900-foot elevation gain, the trail reaches a saddle and a junction. (Mugu Peak Trail on your right is the one to take if time is short and you want to get right to the top of the peak.)

Head north a half mile and gaze over the waves of native grassland. La Jolla Valley really looks like a valley from this perspective because you can see that it's surrounded by peaks and ridges: La Jolla Peak to the north, Boney Mountain to the northeast, and

Laguna Peak (topped by Navy radar and communication apparatus and looking like something from another planet) to the west.

Intersecting La Jolla Valley Loop Trail, go right and make a gentle descent southeast across the grasslands. You'll pass an oak grove, cross a creek, and pass a junction with a left forking trail that extends north across La Jolla Valley. Stay right and soon reach the junction with Mugu Peak Trail.

Mugu Peak Trail travels a ridge above La Jolla Canyon then soon contours around the south slope of the peak.

As for reaching the summit of the peak, a trail rounds the west side of Mugu Peak and another makes some tight aggressive switchbacks up to the peak. Keep your eyes on the prize—the flagpole atop Mugu Peak—and you'll get there just fine.

After enjoying the view, return to the main trail and back to Chumash Trail for the knee-jarring descent to the trailhead.

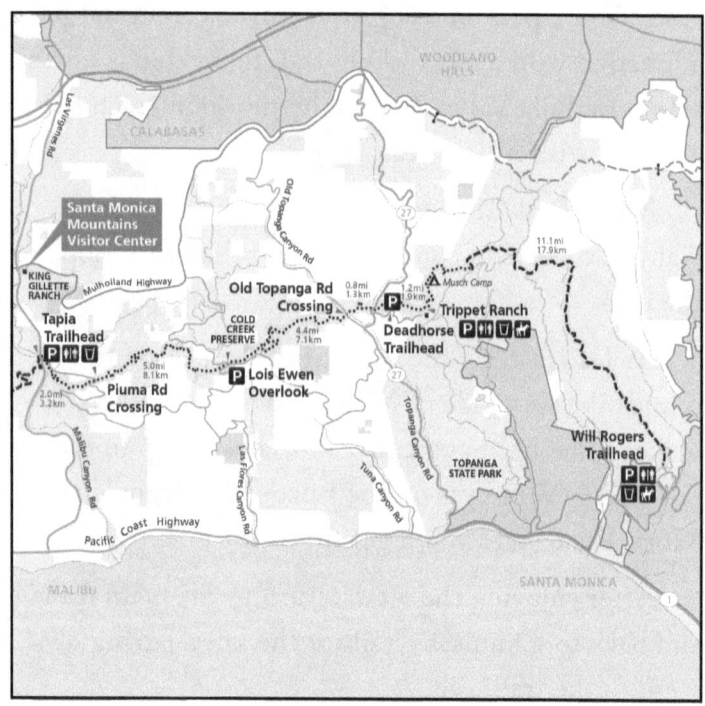

Backbone Trail

If the Backbone Trail were a movie, it would be an epic: decades in the making, dramatic outdoor locations, millions of dollars more to complete than anyone dreamed possible, an armada of government agencies and a cast of thousands.

After more than 40 years of planning, land acquisition, and construction, the trail was completed in 2016. The marquee path, now officially the Backbone National Recreation Trail, extends some 67 miles between Will Rogers State Historic Park and Point Mugu State Park over the spine of the Santa Monica Mountains. The trail passes through three state parks—Topanga, Malibu Creek, Point Mugu—and numerous national parklands.

The trail is gem! Put hiking the Backbone Trail end-to-end on your bucket list.

Overnight camping opportunities are few and far between, so it's best to plan to trek the trail as a series of day hikes. My strategy is to plan one-way hikes

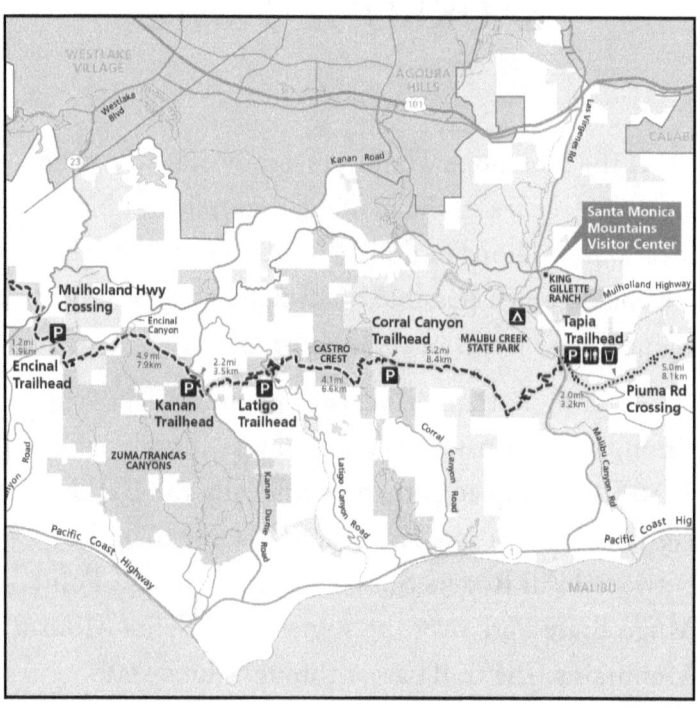

TheTrailmaster.com

and arrange return transport with kind friends or a ride-share service. There are plenty of road-crossings en route so you can choose a distance to cover in a day that matches your time and endurance. A half-dozen hikes in the 10 to 12-mile range is a good way to go. Some hikers like to savor the experience, five or six miles at a time. High-mileage hikers can push through in three or four days.

Five favorite Backbone Trail hikes are featured in this book:

- Between Topanga and Will Rogers parks
- Through Hondo Canyon, complete with a handsome gorge and pinkish-hued sedimentary rock
- Botanically intriguing Dark Canyon and along the boulder strewn top of the range to Saddle Peak
- Through Malibu Creek State Park to Castro Crest
- To Sandstone Peak, highest summit in the Santa Monica Mountains

Expect lots of ups and down en route. That being said, the trail is national park quality, very well engineered with plenty of switchbacks. The trail crosses terrain cloaked in the chaparral and coastal sage flora typical of the mountains. From the ridgelines, hikers

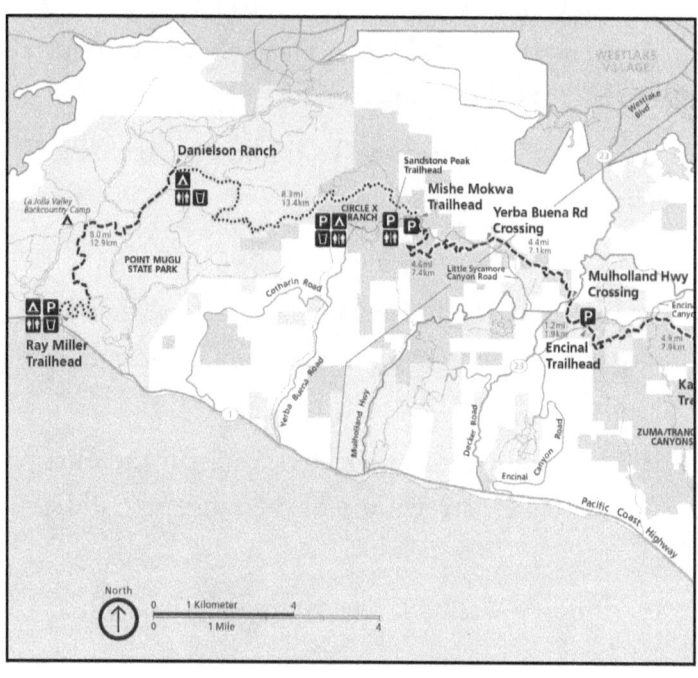

get outstanding views of the metropolis and of the great blue Pacific.

Beginning at the eastern trailhead in Will Rogers or the western trailhead at Point Mugu is strictly a matter of personal preference. My choice is to trek the Backbone from east to west, leaving the city behind and heading for the wild west end of the Santa Monica Mountains. I also like the notion of hiking from the mountains to the sea—from Inspiration Point to the Ray Miller Trailhead located close to the coast.

For the latest Backbone Trail info (guided hikes, trail conditions, fire recovery and more) contact the Santa Monica Mountains National Recreation Area.

JOHN MCKINNEY

John McKinney is the author of 30 books about hiking, parklands and nature, including *Hiking on the Edge: Dreams, Schemes, and 1600 Miles on the California Coastal Trail.*

HIKE Santa Barbara and *HIKE Griffith Park* are among the titles in the The Trailmaster's "Best Day Hikes" series, designed to give hikers the information they need in an engaging and easily accessible way.

For 18 years, he wrote a weekly hiking column for the *Los Angeles Times,* and has hiked and enthusiastically described more than ten thousand miles of trail across America and around the world. John, a.k.a. The Trailmaster, has written more than a thousand articles about hiking plus numerous trail guidebooks in his "Best Day Hikes" series, including regional bestsellers, *HIKE Southern California* and *Day Hiker's Guide to California's State Parks.*

A passionate advocate for hiking and our need to reconnect with nature, John McKinney shares his expertise on radio, TV, online, and as a public speaker.

JOHN MCKINNEY

Hike On.

TheTrailmaster.com

www.ingramcontent.com/pod-product-compliance
Lightning Source LLC
Chambersburg PA
CBHW032042290426
44110CB00012B/910